Beginner's GREEK script

Dennis Couniacis

and

Sheila Hunt

TEACH YOURSELF BOOKS

order queries: please contact Bookpoint Ltd, 78 Milton Park, Abingdon, Oxon
TD. Telephone: (44) 01235 400414, Fax: (44) 01235 400454. Lines are open from
.00, Monday to Saturday, with a 24 hour message answering service.
address: orders@bookpoint.co.uk

   U.S.A. & Canada order queries: please contact NTC/Contemporary Publishing,
55 West Touhy Avenue, Lincolnwood, Illinois 60646–1975, U.S.A.
elephone: (847) 679 5500, Fax: (847) 679 2494.

Long renowned as the authoritative source for self-guided learning – with more than
30 million copies sold worldwide – the *Teach Yourself* series includes over 200 titles in
the fields of languages, crafts, hobbies, business and education.

British Library Cataloguing in Publication Data
A catalogue record for this title is available from The British Library.

Library of Congress Catalog Card Number: On file

First published in UK 2000 by Hodder Headline Plc, 338 Euston Road, London, NW1 3BH.

First published in US 2000 by NTC/Contemporary Publishing, 4255 West Touhy Avenue,
Lincolnwood (Chicago), Illinois 60646–1975 U.S.A.

The 'Teach Yourself' name and logo are registered trade marks of Hodder & Stoughton Ltd.

Copyright © 2000 Dennis Couniacis and Sheila Hunt

Typeset by Transet Limited, Coventry, England.
Printed in Great Britain for Hodder & Stoughton Educational, a division of Hodder
Headline Plc, 338 Euston Road, London NW1 3BH by Cox & Wyman Ltd, Reading,
Berkshire.

Impression number   10 9 8 7 6 5 4 3 2 1
Year   2006 2005 2004 2003 2002 2001 2000

CONTENTS

Prologue _____**vii**

How to use this book _____ viii

Unit 1 | **Taxi** _____ **1**
Seven capital letters: **A, I, M, N, Ξ, O, T,** how to
pronounce them and some handy words they appear in.
Five Greek words to practise the letters given
in this unit.

Unit 2 | **Up and Down**_____ **7**
Seven more capital letters: **Δ, E, Z, K, Π, Y, Ω.**
How it all began – snippets of information about the
history of the Greek alphabet.
False friends – letters which look the same in Greek
and English, but are pronounced differently.
Some useful Greek numerals.
Word practice using all the letters introduced in
Units 1 and 2.

Unit 3 | **A coffee** _____ **18**
Six new capital letters: **Γ, H, Λ, P, Σ, Φ.**
The Greek equivalent of the English 'sh' sound.
Sampling Greek coffee.
How to say 'please'.
Some information about the letter 'B'.
Greek currency.
More Greek numbers you couldn't do without.

Unit 4 | **A drink!** _____ **27**
The last four new capital letters to complete the
Greek alphabet: **B, Θ, X, Ψ.**
The letter combinations **OY, AI, EI, MΠ, TΣ** and **EI.**
Some facts about ouzo.
Eating out in Greece.
Getting around by bus.

Unit 5 | **Time for shopping!** _____ **40**
The letter combinations: **EY**, **OI**, **NT** and **AY**.
A self catering holiday. What to buy, and where to buy it.
The Greek names for some countries.

Glossary (Units 1–5) _____ **50**

Unit 6 | **Shopping!** _____ **59**
Getting used to Greek lower case letters.
Some famous fictional detectives in their Greek and
English forms.
More practice using the combination **ντ**.
Food and drink, and where to buy it, using lower case letters.
The alphabet in capitals, lower case, and with the
Greek letter names.
How modern Greek has developed from its ancient form.
Some headlines from Greek newspapers.
Some English words and their Greek derivations.
Getting used to Greek currency.
Everyday purchases.

Unit 7 | **Eating out** _____ **70**
Greek menus, using lower case letters.
Chips, crisps or potatoes.
Fast food – Greek style.
How to recognise the words for ice cream.

Unit 8 | **At the museum** _____ **78**
The letter combination **TZ** or **τζ**.
Days of the week.
The origin of the 'acropolis'.
Forms of transport using lower case letters.
The ingredients for Greek apple pie.
Different currencies.
Some capital cities.

Unit 9 | **Little trips** _____ **85**
Different uses of the letter **Γ**.
Places to visit.
Days of the week.
Greek newspapers.
Recognising the names of some islands.

Unit 10 | **Souvenirs** _____ **96**

Presents from Greece – food, drink and mementoes.
Greek weather and the words to describe it.
Some Greek acronyms.
Working out Greek prices.
The Greek names of various countries.
How to write postcards in Greek.
A Greek map.
Forms of transport.

Glossary (Units 6–10)_____**109**

Unit 11 | **Useful words** _____**123**

Some useful words to guide you through the potential
minefield of signs, lifts, time, direction and relationships,
when in Greece.

A Brief History of Ancient Greece_____**129**

Unit 12 | **Epilogue** _____**133**

The Greek letter names.
Alphabetical order.
Using a street map.
Using a Greek Dictionary.
Greek–English vocabulary.

English–Greek vocabulary_____**148**

PROLOGUE

Why did we write this book? After all, as you have probably noticed, there are plenty of books that will teach you all the Greek you need, whether it's to enjoy that idyllic holiday or to meet the challenge of A Level. What's new about this book? We'll tell you. This is the only book on the market which helps you to decipher the baffling code which at first sight the Greek script appears to be. We know that 'it's all Greek' to you at the beginning and we give you the written script, so that recognising and pronouncing Greek soon becomes as easy as A, B, C.

'I'm sure I'd enjoy learning Greek, if only there was an easy way to learn the alphabet.'

'I'd really like to learn Greek, if only they didn't have that alphabet.'

If you share the views of Mike and Lisa it's time to let you into a secret. Despite what you may have been told, the Greek alphabet isn't difficult. For a start Greek has only twenty-four letters, and you've coped with learning twenty-six at some time in your life, or you would not be able to read this. Of the twenty-four, about a third are written and pronounced in the same way, whether they are Greek or English, so that cuts down the task still further. Even if you manage to learn only one new letter a day, and with our easy methods you'll probably learn faster than that, you will have enough knowledge to pronounce any Greek letter like a native speaker in slightly over two weeks. Greek, you see, has one enormous advantage over English. Every Greek letter, or letter combination, bar one, has only one way of being pronounced. For example, everybody has heard of the Greek drink **ou**zo, pronounced oozo. The good news is that you always pronounce the **ou** like the 'oo' in moon whenever you meet it in a Greek word, unlike English where you come across thr**ou**gh, th**ou**gh, b**ou**gh, c**ou**gh or en**ou**gh.

Of course, there is still a certain amount to learn, or we wouldn't have written this book. In each chapter we build up your knowledge in small, easily remembered chunks, giving you plenty of practice in pronouncing, reading and writing Greek. You will breeze through situations involving travel, hotels, shops, markets, menus – in fact anywhere that you are likely to meet written Greek. We hope that this book will whet your appetite for this fascinating language, and that you will be keen to go on and learn more!

How to use this book

To help you get the most out of this book we have introduced certain conventions. For easy reference, at the top of every page we have introduced the entire Greek alphabet in capitals. The line underneath shows the new letters in each chapter highlighted in **bold**, as you make progress. After chapter 5 the two lines give you all the capital and lower case letters of the alphabet.

Greek words carry a stress mark which tells you how to pronounce them. The stress mark, however, does not appear until halfway through this book when we tackle the lower case letters.

To help your pronunciation we always highlight in **bold** the letter you stress in a word when that word is written in CAPITALS. Where we use transliteration to help you with the pronunciation, we highlight the stress-carrying letter there instead.

That's all there is to it.

Happy learning.

Dennis Couniacis
Sheila Hunt

1 | ΤΑΞΙ
TAXI

Welcome to the Greek alphabet. We have some good news, some bad news and some more good news to give you.

☺ First, some good news. Do these look familiar?

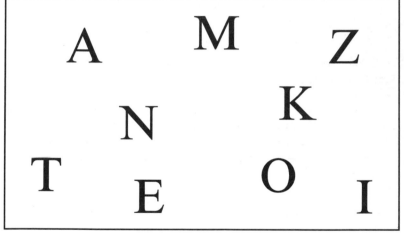

You'll be pleased to know that although they have Greek letter names, these capital letters are pronounced more or less as they are in English. Also, as the Greek alphabet only has 24 and not 26 letters, you already know almost half of them before you start.

In this very first introduction you will join our two novice travellers, Mike and Lisa. Together you will learn how to pronounce Greek words, be introduced to some Greek letters (there are seven altogether in this chapter) and learn how to combine them to pronounce words you have never seen before!

Now some bad news. In the beginning Greek does have some unfamiliar letters which look…well, Greek to you.

Now some more good news. After you get through the first chapter, your ability to read and pronounce Greek will increase very quickly.

In Greek you will encounter three types of letters: 1. letters which look familiar and you may well know already (like those at the top of the page), 2. letters which look familiar but which don't sound like anything you'd expect, and 3. letters which are totally foreign in appearance (like **Π**, **Φ**, and **Ω**) and the pronunciation of which you can't even begin to guess.

The reason for all this confusion lies in Greece's history. Greek is a language that's been around for nearly 3,000 years. It has conquered and been conquered. It has borrowed and been borrowed from and in the process, it has undergone the kind of exciting transformation only a living language is capable of. It is precisely this which makes it both beautiful and infuriating to learn.

Every word you will learn to utter will carry with it the collective sounds of 3,000 years. History will roll off your tongue with every syllable, and, as we all know, history is never straightforward. That's what makes it exciting.

We'll begin our journey into this colourful past with a single word. Appropriately enough, since this is the beginning of our journey (and we kind of just 'stepped' into Greek), we'll begin with the word for taxi. To keep things simple we'll look at the capitals first as it is more likely than not that you'll encounter the word in capitals, anyway.

So step right this way and join Mike as he sticks out a 👍 and flags down a **TAΞI** (TAXI).

Greek pronunciation is pretty much a case of what you see is what you get. That means that each letter has its own individual sound and by stringing them together you can pronounce words you've never seen before.

The **T** in taxi sounds the same as an English *t*.

The **A** sounds like the *a* in **a**pple.

Now here comes the tricky one because the third letter is the 'Ξ'. This is the Greek equivalent of the English 'X' and the sound it makes is the same as the one found in the word 'tax'.

As a matter of fact the first three letters of the Greek word **TAΞI** are pronounced just like the English word 'tax'. Unlike its English equivalent, though, you will never find the Greek 'X' (Ξ) at the end of a word.

The final letter in our first word is **I** pronounced like the *i* sound you expect to find in 'tin' or 'pin.'

Putting the entire word together then, this is what we get:

$$T + A + Ξ + I = t + a + ks + i$$

(The Greek word for: **TAXI**)

> ### ⚑ PIT STOP!
>
> During the reign of Alexander the Great (356–323 BC) Greek was the language of the court and spoken by most of what was then considered the 'civilized' world. Alexander's empire stretched from Greece to India and its creation ushered in the Hellenistic Age, a period of flourishing of the arts and learning that influenced both East and West and outlasted the empire itself.

To help you pronounce Greek better there are marks like this: ´, over the syllable which is stressed. Unfortunately, though, these are used only for the lower case letters. We shall look at them later in the book. For now it is sufficient to know that the word **TAΞI** is pronounced TAXI with the emphasis on the last letter.

So if you had to yell for a taxi in Greece you would need first, to have a good pair of lungs and second, to stress the second syllable of the word TAXI.

Practice

Try practising this on your own for a few minutes. Get your tongue used to making the sound. Remember *i* not *ee*, and stress the second syllable.

Now, just like Mike, you are ready to flag down a taxi in tones almost indistinguishable from those of a native speaker!

Exercise

While Mike was learning how to pronounce 'taxi', Lisa came prepared. She already knows letters which are familiar to her. She knows, for example, that **M** (me) and **N** (nee) are pronounced like... well, *M* and *N* in English. **O** (omicron) is always pronounced with a short *o* as in 'hot'. Because she believes in being prepared, she is practising writing and pronouncing some basic words. See if you can try your hand at this also. Say each of the words below ALOUD several times. Remember, understanding Greek script depends very much upon realising how it all falls together in sentences.

To help you with the exercise we'll tell you that MINI, MONO and NOTA are stressed on the first syllable and MAXI on the second.

MINI (mini) . . . .

MONO (mono) . . . .

NOTA (note) . . . .

ΜΑΞΙ (maxi) . . . .

Remember

MINI – This is a Greek mini. To act Greek you have to say *ni* and not *nee*.

MONO – is pronounced like the first two syllables of **mono**tone – also Greek, but that's another story!

NOTA – as in **not a** drachma more **not a** drachma less!

ΜΑΞΙ – English max + i (not *ee*).

It makes sense!

The sounds of the letters you've just learnt are: **A** = a (as in **a**pple) **M** = m, **N** = n, **O** = o (as in t**o**p), **I** = i (as in p**i**n) and **Ξ** = x (as in ta**x**i). Put the phonetic sound of each letter together and hey presto! You have the word itself.

YOU'VE JUST LEARNT

A – **a**lpha   **Ξ** – **x**ee

I – **y**ota   **O** – **o**micron

M – mee   **T** – taf

N – nee

TOTAL NEW LETTERS: 7
...only 17 letters to go!

Mike and Lisa are novice travellers. In fact this is their first trip outside their country and they're finding things are a little of a rollercoaster ride as they try to get to grips with Greek script.

Things, however, are not all bad. As Lisa already knows, there are many letters in the Greek alphabet which are almost the same as in English. Our next three letters in the Greek alphabet are 'ups' because you will already recognise them:

K (kappa), **E** (epsilon) and **Z** (zeeta)

K makes the same sound as the *k* in **k**ettle, **E** makes the same sound as the *e* in **e**gg and **Z** makes the same sound as the *z* in **z**oo.

Of course, long before **k**ettles came into vogue and it became possible to make a cup of tea for one, it is likely that what was used was a **KAZANI** (ka**z**ani = cauldron)!

Other words where **K** is found which you can instantly pronounce are:

KOMMA (k**o**-ma) = comma (the punctuation mark)

KAKO (ka-k**o**) = bad

KAΔENA (ka-the-na) = neck chain (usually gold rather than silver and one which both men and women can wear.)

There are a lot more words which you can pronounce the moment you lay eyes on them, but before we get to them, we need to come to grips with a 'down' because this is a purely Greek letter:

Ω

You probably noticed this funny looking letter at the end of **ΠANΩ** and **KATΩ**. Greek has two different forms of the letter **O**. One looks just like the English *O* – **O** (**o**micron), and the other looks like **Ω**, the symbol found in a rather expensive make of watches. It's called om**e**ga, (with the stress on the middle syllable), but it sounds exactly like an ordinary *O* as in '**ho**t' and for all practical purposes you can treat it like one.

So now you can go ahead and try to pronounce this word: **KANΩ** (kano).

Say it aloud a couple of times. It means 'I do/I make'.

Ω is the last letter of the Greek alphabet, so now let's skip back to the beginning, or at least as close to it as we can get in this lesson. The fourth letter in the Greek alphabet is **Δ** (pronounced *thelta*), which looks a little like an Egyptian hieroglyph. The similarity is not entirely coincidental. Many of the single letters of the first non-pictorial alphabet were formed

for motive etc

Precursor

by the Semites of Syria between 1500 and 1000 BC. They borrowed their writing from the Egyptians, though – for the sake of simplicity – they dropped many of the single-word characters employed by Egyptian writing and entirely dismissed the pictorial system used by the Egyptian priests. In 1000 BC the Phoenicians created a new alphabet drawn from the Semitic writing system, which had only 22 letters and was thus both easy to learn and easy to use. The Phoenicians were a seafaring nation and they had many dealings with the Greeks along the Mediterranean coastline. The Greek alphabet, which became the forerunner of all Western alphabets, was borrowed from the Phoenician one, though it was, over time, changed quite considerably.

> ### PIT STOP!
>
> When the Greeks borrowed Phoenician writing in about the 9th century BC they made a lot of changes to it. The most important one was the direction of writing. Phoenician writing reads from right to left, as do Hebrew and Arabic which it influenced greatly. Initially, ancient Greek writing would go from right to left and then left to right, changing direction alternatively from line to line. Gradually, however the left to right direction prevailed in the Greek system and in the Western world.

The letter Δ corresponds to the fourth letter in the Phoenician alphabet (*daleth*) and the letter *D* of the Latin alphabet. At one stage, in Greek, Δ did indeed have a *D* sound. This changed over the years to a much softer *th* sound such as that encountered in the English word *'the'* so that the correct modern pronunciation now is *thelta*. You've already encountered it in **KAΔENA** (kathena) and it's used often enough in Greek to be worth its weight in gold!

Try it!

At this point stop and practise saying the letter aloud a few times. This will give you a feel for how it sounds when it's put into words.

Now you're ready to go on.

A   Δ E Z   I K   M N Ξ O Π   T Y   Ω

Here are some words where Δ is used:

ΕΔΩ (e-th-**o**) = here

ΔYO (th**i**-o) = two

ΔΕΞΙΑ (the-xi-**a**) = right (as in the direction)

ΔΕΜΑ (the-ma) = parcel or packet

ΔΕΚΑ (the-ka) = 10

ΔΕΝ (then) = not

The best way to practise these words is to say them aloud a few times.

Todavia está la pelota en el tejado.

You're not quite out of the woods yet. Before we can go ahead and let you loose to talk to the natives we need to point out one more thing. We promised you some 'downs' and here they are.

False friends

(And we don't mean the ones who are after your money).

Because of its historically rich background and the great influence which it has had on the formation of the western alphabet, Greek is full of false friends. These are letters which look familiar, indeed you would swear blind you know what they are, but in reality they sound nothing like what you'd expect. Y (ipsilon) which you met in the word ΔYO is one such false friend.

Despite this, what makes Greek easy to learn is the fact that although there are quite a few letters like that, the sound they make is pretty straightforward. Y is just another I like you'd expect to find in the middle of words like t**i**n, p**i**n and b**i**n. So, whenever you see it, remember it's just another **i**.

How much can you remember?

These are all the words which you have met so far. Can you pronounce them all?

NOTA	TAΞI	MINI	MONO	EΔΩ	KANΩ
ΔYO	ΔEΞIA	ΔEMA	KATΩ	MAΞI	ΔEKA
KOMMA	KAKO	KAΔENA			

Try beating Mike at this game by reading all the words aloud in 10 seconds.

Exercise 1

Now replace the * with letters to complete the puzzle. You will not need all of the words.

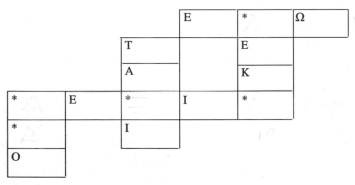

Check at the end of the chapter to see how well you did. If you got most of these, you're on an up which means that you're ready to tackle the last new letter which this chapter has to offer.

Π is called pi and it makes the same sound as *p* in **p**it or **p**ot.

The letter Π is recognisable in the Cyrillic alphabet which is used in Eastern European countries.

Some words which use the letter Π and which you can pronounce are:

ΠΟΤΟ (po-**to**) = drink   ΠΑΝΩ (**pa**no) = up   ΠΙΝΩ (**pi**no) = I drink

ΠΑΩ (**pa**o) = I go   ΠΑΚΕΤΟ (pa**ke**to) = packet

Make it count!

inquietar

Being in a new country has <u>unsettled</u> Mike a little and he has trouble sleeping. To counter this he has decided to do what his grandma always told him to, which is, to count sheep. Being ambitious Mike has decided to do it in Greek! See if you can go one better by reading the numbers below and then doing the exercise.

1 = ENA (**ena**)	2 = ΔYO (th**io**)
6 = EΞI (**eksi**)	7 = EΠTA (ept**a**)
8 = OKTΩ (okt**o**)	9 = ENNEA (en**ea**)
10 = ΔEKA (th**eka**)	12 = ΔΩΔEKA (th**otheka**)
16 = ΔEKAEΞI (theka-**eksi**)	17 = ΔEKAEΠTA (theka-ept**a**)
18 = ΔEKAOKTΩ (theka-okt**o**)	19 = ΔEKAENNEA (theka-en**ea**)

Exercise 2

In the sums below replace the * with the Greek words for the missing numbers.

a	8 + 10 = *		**g**	* × 12 = 12
b	2 + 8 = *		**h**	10 − * = 9
c	12 − 2 = *		**i**	18 − 1 = *
d	18 − 10 = *		**j**	17 + 2 = *
e	8 + * = 10		**k**	8 + 8 = *
f	12 − * = 6		**l**	6 + 1 = *

☺ If you got this far it means that you're now ready to try your hand at identifying useful words and matching them to the pictures in the exercise below.

☺ The even better news is that this time we'll be cruel and won't help you at all! Have a go and see how you do. You have encountered some of the words below in this chapter and the previous one but some are totally new to you. That's how much faith we have in the progress you have made.

Match the words in the box below with the pictures and write the correct answer in the space provided next to each picture.

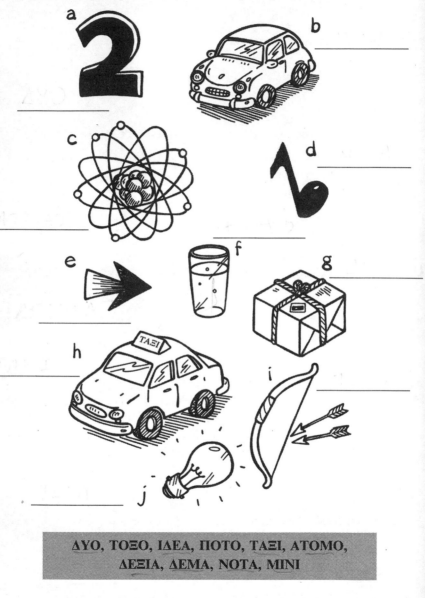

ΔΥΟ, ΤΟΞΟ, ΙΔΕΑ, ΠΟΤΟ, ΤΑΞΙ, ΑΤΟΜΟ, ΔΕΞΙΑ, ΔΕΜΑ, ΝΟΤΑ, ΜΙΝΙ

Hint

As Sherlock once said, 'once you have ruled out the impossible, whatever remains, however improbable must be the correct answer.' To match these begin with the ones you know and then try to make an educated guess at the words which are new to you.

So, how did you do?

The pronunciation of the words is:

ΔEMA – th**e**ma (parcel)

NOTA – n**o**ta (note – musical)

ΔEΞIA – th**e**xi**a** (right – the direction)

MINI – m**i**ni (the cult British car)

ATOMO – **a**tomo (atom)

ΔYO – th**i**o (two)

TAΞI – tax**i** (taxi)

TOΞO – t**o**xo (bow)

IΔEA – ith**e**a (idea)

YOU'VE JUST LEARNT

Δ – thelta (sounds like *th* in **th**en)   Π – pi (sounds like *p* in **p**en)

E – epsilon (sounds like *e* in **e**gg)   Y – ipsilon (sounds like *i* in t**i**n)

K – kappa (like *k* in **k**ettle)   Ω – omega (sounds like *o* in t**o**p)

Z – zeeta (like *z* in **z**oo)

Put these with the letters you learned in chapter 1:

A – alpha

M – mi

N – ni

Ξ – xi

O – omicron

T – taf

I – yota

You can see that in only two chapters, you have learned over half the capital letters in the Greek alphabet.

**TOTAL LETTERS: 14
...only 10 letters to go!**

Any questions ; ; ;

The Greek question mark looks like a semi-colon! Therefore in Greek ; = ?

Solutions

Exercise 1

			E	Δ	Ω
		T		E	
		A		K	
Δ	E	Ξ	I	A	
Y		I			
O					

Exercise 2

a ΔΕΚΑΟΚΤΩ

b ΔΕΚΑ

c ΔΕΚΑ

d ΟΚΤΩ

e ΔΥΟ

f ΕΞΙ

g ΕΝΑ

h ΕΝΑ

i ΔΕΚΑΕΠΤΑ

j ΔΕΚΑΕΝΝΕΑ

k ΔΕΚΑΕΞΙ

l ΕΠΤΑ

3 | ΕΝΑ ΚΑΦΕ
| *A COFFEE*

turismo, excursionismo

If you've been sightseeing all morning like Mike and Lisa have, it's probably time for a break and maybe even a coffee. Coffee breaks are serious business in Greece so you cannot afford to take this one lightly.

By the time we have finished you will be able to order at least three varieties of coffee. You will know how to ask for one which is sweet, you'll learn why there's a Greek letter which looks like the gallows out of *horca* the old game of 'Hangman' and we'll show you a false friend which will blow your socks off!

But let's take things one step at a time. The first letter we tackle in this chapter is none other than:

Φ (phi) = fi

Φ makes exactly the same sound as the letter *f* in **f**avourite, **f**ive and **f**orever or the combination of letters *ph* which are found in words like **ph**ase, **ph**ysiology and **ph**ysics. Knowing that, see if you can now work out what the word opposite is:

ΚΑΦΕ

It's pronounced 'kaffe' – but remember, it's coffee and not a café.

It's not enough however, to just go into a Greek coffee bar and order a coffee.

Before we can satisfactorily explain why, we'll have to throw at least two more letters your way.

The first of these is:

$$\Sigma \text{ (sigma)} = S$$

This letter makes exactly the same sound as S and you will find it in words such as:

ΣΗΜΑ (sima) = sign

ΣΟΚ (sock) = shock

ΣΟΦΙΑ (sofeea) = wisdom

Like most continental languages, Greek tends to borrow English words and transliterate them (like in 'shock'). Unlike in English however there are only 'flat' sounds in Greek, therefore *sh* becomes just another *s* sound, hence the 'sock' pronunciation.

Now unless you're in shock yourself you will have noticed that there is one of those notorious 'false friends' knocking about in one of the words we've just given you.

Take another look at this:
ΣΗΜΑ (sima) = sign.

What looks like the English H in Greek, is actually an *i*! It makes exactly the same sound as any other '*i*' you have met so far, so it makes the sound you'd expect to find in tin, pin, or kit. Contrary to popular perception

---

PIT STOP!

Greece has a very advanced notion of the 'café society'. Coffee bars traditionally were the focal points of the community and every neighbourhood had its own. It would be frequented by the people in the area, much as English neighbourhoods have their 'local' pub, and they would then form a very tightly-knit community. The average length of stay in a traditional coffee bar was not expected to be less than four hours with some patrons easily staying twice as long. Time was passed playing backgammon and cards. As you do not need a special licence in order to sell alcohol in Greece virtually every coffee bar sells alcoholic beverages, which range from beer to whisky, and patrons need not restrict themselves only to coffee!

there is a valid reason why there should be so many letters for the sound *i* in Greek. **I** is by far the most frequently used letter in Greek words (much like the letter *e* in English). Inevitably then there are some words which, when pronounced, sound exactly the same (they're homophones, to use a word borrowed from the Greeks) but have different meanings. In order to differentiate between them, it became necessary to be able to write them with a different spelling, hence the different varieties of the letter *i*.

Back to the task though.

The next vital letter you need to complete your journey towards the promised cup of coffee in this chapter is:

Λ (lamda) = L

Λ makes the same sound as the English *L*, so although it looks very different it is actually very easy to use.

Some words which use the letter **Λ** are:

ΛΑΟΣ (la**o**s) = people, race   ΛΑΔΙ (l**a**thi) = oil

ΕΛΕΟΣ (**e**leos) = mercy   ΠΟΛΥ (p**o**li) = very

ΕΛΛΗΝΙΚΟΣ (elinik**o**s) = Greek

The last word here is particularly useful as it is also used to refer to a very special type of coffee. Greek coffee is served in a thick, short half-cup (the French call it *demitasse*). It is usually served sweet or very sweet and it is never drunk with milk! If you are tempted to order Greek coffee at all (and you should at least once – it is an experience) be warned. It should be sipped delicately rather than gulped down. The reason for this is that it is brewed from coffee powder which is ground while the coffee beans are still fresh and only then is it lightly roasted. That means that in order for it to be made into coffee it has to be brought to the boil slowly in an old-fashioned, stove-top coffee pot and then poured into a cup. The brewing process produces some very throat-clogging dregs which are poured into the coffee cup along with the coffee and they settle to form a thick sediment at the bottom of the cup. Gulp your coffee instead of sipping it and you will immediately see the wisdom (ΣΟΦΙΑ) of always having a glass of water served with coffee in Greece.

Coffee, sweet coffee!

We're almost there now and we know you can practically smell the coffee, which is why we've left it until now to introduce the final letter you will need before you can order your coffee in Greek. At the beginning of this chapter we warned you that it looked like something you'd expect to see in a game of 'hangman'. If you played the same type of 'hangman' as we did, then you won't be surprised to see that the letter is:

Γ

It looks a little like the gallows and it is called gamma. Usually it can be pronounced as **wh**, except when it is followed by an **i** (any **i** and in Greek there are six!), in which case, it makes the sound **y**, as in **y**esterday, **y**ellow and **y**es.

The reason we're learning it now is because the word 'sweet' begins with it:

ΓΛΥΚΟ (whlik**o**) = sweet

This is a very easy word to remember because the word glucose actually comes from it.

🔑 PIT STOP!

Gamma began life looking exactly like the L-plates of learner drivers today. It was stood on its head and reversed by the Semites at around 1500 BC. The Semites made it linear and thought it looked like a throwing stick. They called it gimel or gaml, meaning 'throwing stick'. The Greeks changed the Semitic name to gamma and, when they began to write from left to right, reversed the direction it was facing so that it looked like a gallows, as it does today.

Other words which use it are: ΓΑΛΑ (wh-**a**la) = milk

ΓΙΑΤΙ (ya**ti**) = why

ΓΙΑ (ya) = for

In the introduction we mentioned that every Greek letter or letter combination, bar one, has only one way of being pronounced. Well, this is *the* one. Γ does some rather funny things to your vocal chords as you will see later on. You've been warned!

Coffee at last!

punto decisivo

And now the <u>crunch</u>. We brought you all this way in the alphabet so you can finally order coffee on your own. There are quite a few ways you can order coffee in Greece, but since we've just learnt about it we'll opt for the cultural experience and go for a Greek one. Remember, let it settle after it arrives and sip it delicately!

In the exercise below you'll have to replace the pictures, symbols and English words with Greek words you have learnt in order to place your order:

A) **1**

B) **1**

C) **1**

chortes

Two coffees

There is an anecdotal story making the rounds which recounts how Greece's Prime Minister during WWII, Yannis Metaxas, a man renowned for his quips, was once asked during a pre-election campaign by one of Athens' famous coffee house proprietors, what could possibly be better than a cup of Greek coffee to revitalise a person in the morning. Without batting an eyelid he replied: 'Two coffees'.

Now, in case you feel the same way, we will help you order more than one.

In English most words which refer to more than one item (plural) simply have -s or -es added to the end. Greek however (you'll be surprised to know), is not that straightforward. Although there are grammatical rules explaining when and how (we won't bother you with those), the reasons for it lie mainly in the phonetics of the language and the need to distinguish between endings which would sound virtually identical in the single and plural form of a word.

> ### ⚑ PIT STOP!
>
> The magic word 'please' and its response are not much used in Greece. This is a cultural difference. People in Greece are very casual and laid back when dealing with one another and foreigners. As a result they tend to view excessive politeness as a distancing device and therefore avoid using it. When they say 'Please' and 'Thank you' they really mean it. It is not just a convention of the language.

Coffee then, which is **ΚΑΦΕ** becomes **ΚΑΦΕΔΕΣ**.

Knowledge almost always comes with some form of responsibility attached. And having now given you the word for coffees, we want to see you exercise it by writing out in Greek the English sentences given to you below.

More than one

1 Two coffees

....

2 Six coffees

....

3 Ten coffees

....

Water!

If you took our advice, waited patiently for your Greek coffee to settle after it was brought to you and then sipped it delicately, the chances are you have enjoyed a fine cultural experience. If, however, you didn't, then we know that you'll need a little more than just the one glass of water which came with your coffee. To prepare you to ask for more, we introduce our final letter in this chapter, which, as things go, is probably the worst false friend you're likely to see:

P

We know it looks like a *p*. It isn't!

The letter in Greek is pronounced *rho* and it makes the sound *r* as in **r**iver, **r**over and **r**ivet.

The word water in Greek is: **ΝΕΡΟ**

It is pronounced ne**r**o and the plural (just in case) is **ΝΕΡΑ** (ne**r**a) and yes, you can ask for two waters in Greek as opposed to two glasses of water.

> ## ⚑ PIT STOP!
>
> Nine times out of ten a waiter's response to an order is ΑΜΕΣΩΣ (amesos) – literally meaning 'immediately'. This is just a turn of phrase. Waiters in Greece are notorious for taking far too many orders at once and keeping customers waiting for some time. The Greeks accept this and use the time to chat and people-watch.

The magic word

Now that you've learnt the letter **P** you can learn the 'magic word' in Greek:

ΠΑΡΑΚΑΛΩ = please (parakalo)

Mike and Lisa are unaware of the cultural differences they encounter on their first holiday abroad. They order coffee using 'please' as they would back at home. See if you can order again using the word 'please' this time.

1 Two coffees please

....

2 Six coffees please

....

3 Ten coffees please

....

The good news now is that with so many of the 'difficult' letters under your belt you're adept enough in Greek to see that words like ΑΓΟΡΑ (pronounced *awhora* – we know it's not *ayora,* don't say we didn't warn you about gamma) must have some connection to agoraphobia (fear of open spaces). ΑΓΟΡΑ, in fact, means marketplace (in ancient Greece this was indeed an open space in the middle of the city. All commercial activity took place there).

It also gives you the word: **ΑΓΟΡΑΖΩ** (awhora**z**o) = I buy.

If your taste runs to something stronger than a coffee, you'll have to wait until our next chapter where we will join Mike and Lisa as they begin to think about drinks!

YOU'VE JUST LEARNT

H = ita	**Λ** = lamda
Φ = phi	**Γ** = gamma
Σ = sigma	**P** = rho

TOTAL NEW LETTERS: 6
*You now know 20 letters
altogether. Only 4 letters left!*

Solutions

Coffee at last!

A. ENA KAΦE

B. ENA ΓΛΥΚΟ ΚΑΦΕ

C. ENA ΠΟΛΥ ΓΛΥΚΟ ΚΑΦΕ

More than one

1 ΔΥΟ ΚΑΦΕΔΕΣ

2 ΕΞΙ ΚΑΦΕΔΕΣ

3 ΔΕΚΑ ΚΑΦΕΔΕΣ

The magic word

1 ΔΥΟ ΚΑΦΕΔΕΣ ΠΑΡΑΚΑΛΩ

2 ΕΞΙ ΚΑΦΕΔΕΣ ΠΑΡΑΚΑΛΩ

3 ΔΕΚΑ ΚΑΦΕΔΕΣ ΠΑΡΑΚΑΛΩ

4 | ΕΝΑ ΠΟΤΟ!
A DRINK!

Tired and thirsty from doing the tourist bit, Mike is now ready for a stiff drink. Greeks share the Mediterranean penchant for drinking at any part of the day, though never to excess, and in this chapter we shall look at emulating them. Unlike Mike you will get a lot of practice ordering a vast variety of drinks, learn about a place where you can order them (more about that in a moment), come to grips with the final letters of the Greek alphabet and learn about some combinations of Greek letters which are bound to have you ordering doubles!

Since you're fresh, strong and eager here's the first one:

OY

This letter combination makes exactly the same sound you'd expect to find in **Zoo** and, handily enough, it is found in the Greek word

OYZO (oozo)

OYZO is made from the piths of grapes after wine makers have finished with them and it is indicative of the native genius for letting few things go to waste. When it is distilled it is a clear, odourless liquid which looks a lot like water. To flavour it, OYZO makers have always used aniseed which gives it its characteristic OYZO taste.   *grano de anis*

The extract from the aniseed plant (*Pimpinella anisum*) is poisonous in any quantity, however in the minuscule amounts used in OYZO all it does is impart the characteristic liquorice taste and also goes cloudy when water is added to it.

Bottled OYZO is sold practically anywhere in Greece, from the local Deli to the larger supermarket and everywhere in between. You can drink OYZO though in places like a café and a taverna. The Greeks however never drink without eating and every place which offers drinks is obliged to also offer some food in order to attract clientele. Traditionally, small fishing villages and poor neighbourhoods lacked the wealth necessary for the setting up and sustaining of large restaurants. To meet the need for something small, a new class of drinking establishment arose called OYZEPI (oozeri) – literally a place where one could go to drink OYZO.

Exercise 1

Below we give you a number of other drinks you can buy at an OYZEPI along with their pronunciations and English counterparts. See if you can match them by tracing lines which join the Greek word with its pronunciation and its meaning.

OYZO	wh-**a**la	water
KΡΑΣΙ	mart**i**ni	lemonade
NEPO	oo**i**ski	whisky
TEKIΛA	portokal**a**tha	tequila
OYIΣKI	lemon**a**tha	milk
MAPTINI	ner**o**	wine
ΓΑΛΑ	kras**i**	martini
ΛEMONAΔA	tek**i**la	ouzo
ΠOPTOKAΛAΔA	**oo**zo	orangeade

Never on an empty stomach

Although OYZEPI were (and still are) drinking establishments they do offer food on a very limited basis. The reasons why the menu is limited are to be found in the reasons OYZEPI first came into existence in the first place: mainly the lack of money necessary to sustain anything larger. OYZEPI today are trendy establishments found all over mainland Greece and the islands. They are there mainly for the locals though more and more tourists have begun to discover them. Reflecting their origins OYZEPI offer two kinds of food: dairy products and sea food.

Try practising saying the words below aloud:

ΜΕΖΕΣ
ΣΑΓΑΝΑΚΙ
ΟΚΤΑΠΟΔΙ
ΚΕΦΤΕΔΑΚΙΑ
ΠΑΤΑΤΕΣ

That's just the kind of fare you will find on the menu of an OUZEPI. Now see how successful you were at deciphering the pronunciation.

ΜΕΖΕΣ (mezes) = a mixed platter which normally contains a couple of meatballs, chips, a sausage and fried goat's cheese.

ΣΑΓΑΝΑΚΙ (sa-wh-anaki) = fried goat's cheese. A delicacy in Greece.

ΟΚΤΑΠΟΔΙ (oktapothi) = octopus, standard sea-food fare in fishing villages. These are marinated to make them tender and shallow fried for a virtually unique taste.

ΚΕΦΤΕΔΑΚΙΑ (keftethakia) = small meatballs.

ΠΑΤΑΤΕΣ (patates) = nothing more than the very familiar chips.

On the bus

Mike has decided to do a little local travelling in order to get to the various eating and drinking places near where he is staying, but before he can do that he has to be able to distinguish one food from another and for that to happen, he has to come to grips with a new letter combination:

EI

EI may look hard to make head or tail of, but the sound it makes is simply *i*, just as you'd find in pick, sit and drink. It is found in the word for bus:

ΛΕΩΦΟΡΕΙΟ (leoforio) = bus

Now that you know how to recognise a bus there is nothing to stop you from joining Mike as he sets out for an evening's eating out.

I want

Knowing the menu, being able to pronounce with confidence what is on it and order a variety of drinks to wash it down with means that the time has come to learn a brand new letter!

The letter in this case is:

Θ

It is called theta. It makes the sound you'd expect to find in English words like **the**sis, **the**saurus and **the**atre.

Now that you know it you can try using the following word: ΘΕΛΩ = I want.

Because Greek verbs have different endings for whoever is performing an action you don't have to worry about learning extra words such as I, you etc.

So:

ΘΕΛΩ	(**the**lo)	I want
ΘΕΛΕΙΣ	(**the**lis)	You want
ΘΕΛΕΙ	(**the**li)	He/She/It wants
ΘΕΛΟΥΜΕ	(**the**loome)	We want
ΘΕΛΕΤΕ	(**the**lete)	You want
ΘΕΛΟΥΝΕ	(**the**loone)	They want

☺ The good news is that now you can form sentences such as 'I want an ouzo with meze' with the same ease as native speakers, provided of course you have a couple of linking words to hand, otherwise you will be doomed never to get anything **with** something else!

predestinado

So, final deep breath and here goes.

The two words you need in order to make your culinary experience complete are:

KAI and ME

The first thing you've noticed are the letters **AI**. Before they start to affect your appetite we can tell you that they're easy to pronounce. The letter combination together makes the sound *e* such as you'd find in tender, tepid and trepidation.

That means that the word KAI is pronounced *ke* and it means 'and'.

KAI (ke) = and

The next word is even easier:

ME (mae) = with

The word is pronounced exactly the same as the first syllable of **me**tal.

☺ The good news now is that there is nothing to stop you from ordering a hearty Greek meal.

Exercise 2

In the exercise below the Greek and English sentences have somehow become mixed up. See if you can unravel them by replacing the English words with Greek. *desenmarañar*

1 ΘΕΛΩ ΕΝΑ ΟΥΖΟ WITH WATER KAI MEZE

2 ΘΕΛΟΥΜΕ CHIPS WITH ΚΕΦΤΕΔΑΚΙΑ

3 ΘΕΛΟΥΜΕ ΕΝΑ ΣΑΓΑΝΑΚΙ KAI TWO MARTINIS

4 ΔΥΟ ΠΑΤΑΤΕΣ KAI ΕΝΑ OCTOPUS PLEASE

5 THREE WHISKIES ΔΥΟ ΠΑΤΑΤΕΣ KAI ΕΝΑ MEZE ΠΑΡΑΚΑΛΩ

6 I WANT AN OUZO ME NEPO AND MEZE

7 WE WANT ΠΑΤΑΤΕΣ ME MEATBALLS

8 WE WANT COOKED GOAT'S CHEESE AND ΔΥΟ ΜΑΡΤΙΝΙ

9 TWO CHIPS AND ONE ΟΚΤΑΠΟΔΙ ΠΑΡΑΚΑΛΩ

10 ΤΡΙΑ ΟΥΙΣΚΙ TWO CHIPS AND ONE MEZE PLEASE

Α Β Γ Δ Ε Ζ Η Θ Ι Κ Λ Μ Ν Ξ Ο Π Ρ Σ Τ Υ Φ Χ Ψ Ω

How about a bottle?

Generally speaking drinks are a lot cheaper in Greece than they are in England, so it would be a good idea to start ordering bottles of everything! Before you can do that however we'll have to tell you that there is no individual letter sound for *B* in Greek. Greek gets round the problem by combining two letters to form the sound it needs:

$$\text{ΜΠ} = \text{the English letter } B$$

Now perhaps you can make some sense of the following signs:

ΜΠΑΡ (bar) = bar	ΜΠΟΥΚΑΛΙ (bookali) = bottle
ΜΠΥΡΑ (bira) = beer	ΜΠΟΥΚΑΛΙΑ (bookalia) = bottles

In Greek when you want to say 'a bottle of' something, all you need to do is put the words 'one bottle' in front of what you want. A bottle of ouzo, for example, becomes ΕΝΑ ΜΠΟΥΚΑΛΙ ΟΥΖΟ.

Exercise 3

Mike is a fast learner. Already he has got into the habit of buying bottles of everything. In the exercise below, see if you can replace the English sentences with Greek ones.

1 Ten bottles of beer please.
2 Six bottles of wine please.
3 Two bottles of whisky please.
4 One bottle of water please.

Greek uses a few more letter combinations to make single-letter sounds:

ΟΥ – **ΟΥΖΟ**	makes the sound -*oo*
ΕΙ – **ΘΕΛΕΙΣ**	makes the sound -*i*
ΑΙ – **ΚΑΙ**	makes the sound -*e*
ΤΣ – **ΠΙΤΣΑ** (pizza)	makes the sound -*ts*

Exercise 4

Entertainment is never to be taken lightly in Greek society. Because of this, a certain specialisation has taken place in places which provide different types of food and drink. Mike wants to go out to get something to eat, but he has forgotten where he is most likely to find what. See if you can help him by matching the establishment with its identifying food or drink!

ΠΙΤΣΑΡΙΑ	ΟΥΖΟ
ΟΥΖΕΡΙ	ΚΑΦΕΣ
ΚΑΦΕΤΕΡΙΑ	ΠΙΤΣΑ
ΜΠΥΡΑΡΙΑ	ΜΠΥΡΑ

> You'll probably notice that coffee now appears as ΚΑΦΕΣ. Greek nouns have a number of forms that necessitate the usage of 's' at the end, or conversely the dropping of it. We promised you that this would be fun, so no grammar, which means you'll have to take our word for it! If you do get it wrong, at this stage, Greeks will understand what you are saying, so no harm done.

A bite to eat

When it comes to eating places, the one most people will have heard of the most of course is a taverna. Greek tavernas were the original restaurants. Their menus changed according to what was in season and they served wine drawn directly from a barrel and served in either half litre or litre tin containers – a practice still carried out today. Tellingly, perhaps, a taverna's reputation (and therefore its success) could be made or broken by the quality of its wine rather than its food. Good tavernas would have up to eight different types of wine to draw from. The reason we left it until now, however, is because the tourists' favourite eating place in Greece, when written, displays a 'false friend':

ΤΑΒΕΡΝΑ = taverna

PIT STOP!

The letter B forms part of the name of the English word 'alphabet'. It was borrowed by the Greeks from the Canaanites around 1000 BC. The Canaanites used a linear form of B adapted from Egyptian hieroglyphics and they called it 'beth', literally meaning 'house'. At that time it stood for a stylised picture of a house. The Greeks changed 'beth' to 'beta' and from there it entered, unchanged, into the Latin alphabet and then the English.

Α Β Γ Δ Ε Ζ Η Θ Ι Κ Λ Μ Ν Ξ Ο Π Ρ Σ Τ Υ Φ Χ Ψ Ω

Β (beta) = veeta

The letter **Β** in Greek, at one stage did actually sound like the English *B*. For a variety of reasons, over the years, it was softened from the original beta to **veeta** and its sound, accordingly, changed from *B* to *V*.

Other words which use the letter **Β** are:

ΒΙΒΛΙΟ (vivlio) = book

ΒΑΖΟ (vazo) = vase

ΒΟΥΤΗΡΟ (vootiro) = butter

Pay up!

The Greek currency is the drachma. You will have to use it while in the country so it would be a good idea to learn how to say it. This gives us the opportunity to tackle the last one of those 'false friends':

Χ = hee

While it looks exactly like the English *X* this Greek letter is actually an *H*! It makes exactly the kind of sound you'd find in words like **H**imalaya, **h**ibiscus and **h**ibernation.

It is also, rather conveniently, found in the word ΔΡΑΧΜΗ (pronounced *Thrahmee*) – the drachma.

When there's more than one ΔΡΑΧΜΗ the plural is ΔΡΑΧΜΕΣ (*thrahmes*) and in shops, on price tags it will most often appear in its truncated form of: ΔΡΧ.

More numbers

2 = ΔΥΟ

3 = ΤΡΕΙΣ

100 = ΕΚΑΤΟ

1000 = ΧΙΛΙΑ

2000 = ΔΥΟ ΧΙΛΙΑΔΕΣ

Exercise 5

In the exercise below match the prices Mike has to pay with the price tags:

ΔΥΟ ΧΙΛΙΑΔΕΣ ΔΡΑΧΜΕΣ
(thio hiliathes thrahmes)   1000 ΔΡΧ

ΕΞΙ ΧΙΛΙΑΔΕΣ
(exi hiliathes thrahmes)   10 000 ΔΡΧ

ΔΕΚΑ ΧΙΛΙΑΔΕΣ ΔΡΑΧΜΕΣ
(theka hiliathes thrahmes)   3000 ΔΡΧ

ΕΚΑΤΟ ΧΙΛΙΑΔΕΣ ΔΡΑΧΜΕΣ
(ekato hiliathes thrahmes)   2000 ΔΡΧ

ΧΙΛΙΕΣ ΔΡΑΧΜΕΣ
(hilies thrahmes)   6000 ΔΡΧ

ΤΡΕΙΣ ΧΙΛΙΑΔΕΣ ΔΡΑΧΜΕΣ
(tris hiliathes thrahmes)   100 000 ΔΡΧ

Something fishy

With this letter you will have learnt the whole Greek alphabet:

$$Ψ = psi$$

This letter makes exactly the kind of sound you'd expect to find in English words like har**psi**cord and Pe**psi**.

Greek words which use this letter include:

ΨΑΡΙ (ps**a**ri) = fish
ΨΩΜΙ (ps**o**mi) = bread
ΨΩΝΙΖΩ (ps**o**nizo) = I buy

Α Β Γ Δ Ε Ζ Η Θ Ι Κ Λ Μ Ν Ξ Ο Π Ρ Σ Τ Υ Φ Χ Ψ Ω

In a word

Greek society and culture is quite literal. Often occupations and jobs are made of compound words which describe exactly what goes on. So, a baker for example would be a 'breadmaker', while a fish-seller would be … a fish-seller!

The Greek word for 'I sell' is: ΠΟΥΛΩ (poul**o**). This is slightly (but only slightly) modified when combined with other words.

Exercise 6

Match the product with the place that sells it.

ΨΑΡΙ (ps**a**ri) = fish   ΦΡΟΥΤΟΠΩΛΕΙΟ

ΦΡΟΥΤΑ (fr**oo**ta) = fruit   ΤΥΡΟΠΩΛΕΙΟ

ΤΥΡΙ (t**i**ri) = cheese   ΓΑΛΑΚΤΟΠΩΛΕΙΟ

ΓΑΛΑ (wh-**a**la) = milk   ΨΑΡΟΠΩΛΕΙΟ

More good news is that now, armed with the entire Greek alphabet as we are, there is nothing to stop us going shopping!

YOU'VE JUST LEARNT

ΟΥ ou – *oo* as in z**oo**

ΕΙ epsilon yota – *i* as in p**i**t

Θ theta – *th* as in **th**istle

ΑΙ alpha yota – *e* as in **e**lephant

ΜΠ mi pi – *b* as in **b**eer

ΤΣ taf sigma – *ts* as in le**ts**

Β veeta – *v* as in **v**ase

Χ hee – *h* as in **h**en

Ψ psi – *psi* as in Pe**psi**

CONGRATULATIONS!
*You now know all the letters of
the Greek alphabet!*

Solutions

Exercise 1

ΟΥΖΟ	oozo	ouzo
ΚΡΑΣΙ	krasi	wine
ΝΕΡΟ	nero	water
ΤΕΚΙΛΑ	tekila	tequila
ΟΥΙΣΚΙ	ooiski	whisky
ΜΑΡΤΙΝΙ	martini	martini
ΓΑΛΑ	wh-ala	milk
ΛΕΜΟΝΑΔΑ	lemonatha	lemonade
ΠΟΡΤΟΚΑΛΑΔΑ	portokalatha	orangeade

Exercise 2

1 ΘΕΛΩ ΕΝΑ ΟΥΖΟ ΜΕ ΝΕΡΟ ΚΑΙ ΜΕΖΕ
2 ΘΕΛΟΥΜΕ ΠΑΤΑΤΕΣ ΜΕ ΚΕΦΤΕΔΑΚΙΑ
3 ΘΕΛΟΥΜΕ ΕΝΑ ΣΑΓΑΝΑΚΙ ΚΑΙ ΔΥΟ ΜΑΡΤΙΝΙ
4 ΔΥΟ ΠΑΤΑΤΕΣ ΚΑΙ ΕΝΑ ΟΚΤΑΠΟΔΙ ΠΑΡΑΚΑΛΩ
5 ΤΡΙΑ ΟΥΙΣΚΙ ΔΥΟ ΠΑΤΑΤΕΣ ΚΑΙ ΕΝΑ ΜΕΖΕ
ΠΑΡΑΚΑΛΩ
6 ΘΕΛΩ ΕΝΑ ΟΥΖΟ ΜΕ ΝΕΡΟ ΚΑΙ ΜΕΖΕ
7 ΘΕΛΟΥΜΕ ΠΑΤΑΤΕΣ ΜΕ ΚΕΦΤΕΔΑΚΙΑ
8 ΘΕΛΟΥΜΕ ΣΑΓΑΝΑΚΙ ΚΑΙ ΔΥΟ ΜΑΡΤΙΝΙ
9 ΔΥΟ ΠΑΤΑΤΕΣ ΚΑΙ ΕΝΑ ΟΚΤΑΠΟΔΙ ΠΑΡΑΚΑΛΩ
10 ΤΡΙΑ ΟΥΙΣΚΙ ΔΥΟ ΠΑΤΑΤΕΣ ΚΑΙ ΕΝΑ ΜΕΖΕ
ΠΑΡΑΚΑΛΩ

Exercise 3

1 ΔΕΚΑ ΜΠΟΥΚΑΛΙΑ ΜΠΥΡΑ ΠΑΡΑΚΑΛΩ
2 ΕΞΙ ΜΠΟΥΚΑΛΙΑ ΚΡΑΣΙ ΠΑΡΑΚΑΛΩ
3 ΔΥΟ ΜΠΟΥΚΑΛΙΑ ΟΥΙΣΚΙ ΠΑΡΑΚΑΛΩ
4 ΕΝΑ ΜΠΟΥΚΑΛΙ ΝΕΡΟ ΠΑΡΑΚΑΛΩ

Exercise 4

ΠΙΤΣΑΡΙΑ	ΠΙΤΣΑ
ΟΥΖΕΡΙ	ΟΥΖΟ
ΚΑΦΕΤΕΡΙΑ	ΚΑΦΕΣ
ΜΠΥΡΑΡΙΑ	ΜΠΥΡΑ

Exercise 5

ΔΥΟ ΧΙΛΙΑΔΕΣ ΔΡΑΧΜΕΣ (thio hiliathes thrahmes)	2000 ΔΡΧ
ΕΞΙ ΧΙΛΙΑΔΕΣ (exi hiliathes thrahmes)	6000 ΔΡΧ
ΔΕΚΑ ΧΙΛΙΑΔΕΣ ΔΡΑΧΜΕΣ (theka hiliathes thrahmes)	10 000 ΔΡΧ
ΕΚΑΤΟ ΧΙΛΙΑΔΕΣ ΔΡΑΧΜΕΣ (ekato hiliathes thrahmes)	100 000 ΔΡΧ
ΧΙΛΙΕΣ ΔΡΑΧΜΕΣ (hilies thrahmes)	1000 ΔΡΧ
ΤΡΕΙΣ ΧΙΛΙΑΔΕΣ ΔΡΑΧΜΕΣ (tris hiliathes thrahmes)	3000 ΔΡΧ

Exercise 6

ΨΑΡΙ (psari) = fish   ΨΑΡΟΠΩΛΕΙΟ

ΦΡΟΥΤΑ (froota) = fruit   ΦΡΟΥΤΟΠΩΛΕΙΟ

ΤΥΡΙ (tiri) = cheese   ΤΥΡΟΠΩΛΕΙΟ

ΓΑΛΑ (wh-ala) = milk   ΓΑΛΑΚΤΟΠΩΛΕΙΟ

5 | ΩΡΑ ΓΙΑ ΨΩΝΙΑ!
TIME FOR SHOPPING!

OK! We know that the heading here is hard. Nevertheless we are so confident there is nothing you cannot deal with that we are prepared to take you shopping! The word for 'I shop' in Greek is:

ΨΩΝΙΖΩ = psonizo

And the word for the things you buy, unsurprisingly, is:

ΨΩΝΙΑ = psonia

Before we take you shopping however we will throw one more new word at you:

ΜΑΓΑΖΙ (ma-wh-azi) – shop

Exercise 1

Mike, who is self-catering needs to buy some food. He has a complete list of things to buy. Unfortunately his list is in English. Perhaps you could help him by matching up the English on his list with the Greek equivalent.

Bread	ΠΟΡΤΟΚΑΛΑΔΑ
Cheese	ΛΑΔΙ
Beer	ΖΑΧΑΡΗ
Coffee	ΤΥΡΙ
Sugar	ΟΥΙΣΚΙ
Retsina	ΚΑΦΕΣ
Milk	ΨΩΜΙ

Oil (to cook with)
Whisky
Orangeade

ΜΠΥΡΑ

ΓΑΛΑ

ΡΕΤΣΙΝΑ

Exercise 2

Now Mike faces another problem. He has to decide where he can buy the items he needs. Once again he has to rely on your help to guide him. See if you can link the Greek items on the left with the places where they could be found on the right.

1	ΠΟΡΤΟΚΑΛΑΔΑ	ΣΟΥΠΕΡΜΑΡΚΕΤ
2	ΛΑΔΙ	
3	ΖΑΧΑΡΗ	
4	ΤΥΡΙ	
5	ΟΥΙΣΚΙ	ΤΥΡΟΠΩΛΕΙΟ
6	ΚΑΦΕΣ	
7	ΨΩΜΙ	
8	ΜΠΥΡΑ	ΓΑΛΑΚΤΟΠΩΛΕΙΟ
9	ΓΑΛΑ	
10	ΡΕΤΣΙΝΑ	

Exercise 3

While shopping for the items on his list Mike has met Lisa who is also on a self-catering holiday. They have struck up a friendship and he is now planning to take her out. The problem is that he cannot remember where they can be expected to serve what. See if you can help him by drawing lines matching up the food and drinks on the left with the place where they serve them on the right.

Α Β Γ Δ Ε Ζ Η Θ Ι Κ Λ Μ Ν Ξ Ο Π Ρ Σ Τ Υ Φ Χ Ψ Ω

1 ΚΑΦΕΣ | ΟΥΖΕΡΙ |

2 ΠΟΡΤΟΚΑΛΑΔΑ

3 ΜΕΖΕΣ | ΤΑΒΕΡΝΑ |

4 ΟΥΖΟ

5 ΚΡΑΣΙ | ΚΑΦΕΤΕΡΙΑ |

6 ΜΠΥΡΑ

7 ΠΙΤΣΑ

8 ΠΑΤΑΤΕΣ | ΜΠΥΡΑΡΙΑ |

9 ΣΑΓΑΝΑΚΙ

10 ΚΕΦΤΕΔΑΚΙΑ | ΠΙΤΣΑΡΙΑ |

Shopping

We mentioned in Unit 3 that Greek has given us the word agoraphobia
(fear of open spaces). The original market place where shopping of all
kinds took place in ancient Greece was an open space called Agora
(ΑΓΟΡΑ). Open-air markets are a weekly feature of Greek urban life.
While traditionally you find fresh produce there at very reasonable prices,
these days, you can also buy cheap watches, videos and cassettes!

Haggling is a feature of buying associated more closely with life on the
Greek islands (a remnant of their barter economy) than any market place
on the Greek mainland. You are not traditionally expected to haggle when
you are buying gifts. However, certain tourist spots, like Corfu and
Rhodes, do pander to this by artificially inflating their prices. The best
way to decide whether you can haggle at a place or not is to shop around
and compare prices, like you would at home.

Exercise 4

Mike has discovered that drinks in Greece are indeed cheaper. He has invited Lisa to visit him in his flat and, being the perfect host, he needs to have a drink or two to offer her. He has splashed out on some drinks which are in a jumble below. Decide which drinks Mike bought. If you are right the letters going down the bottle will tell you which one he did not buy because he couldn't ask for it!

			K		–	Σ	I
			N		P	O	
–	A	P		–	I	N	I
O	Y	–		–	K	–	
T	E	–		–	Λ	A	
–	E	M	O	–	A	–	–
		Γ		–		A	

ΚΡΑΣΙ, ΓΑΛΑ, ΛΕΜΟΝΑΔΑ, ΜΑΡΤΙΝΙ, ΟΥΙΣΚΙ, ΤΕΚΙΛΑ, ΝΕΡΟ

Manners please!

Now that we have learnt about culture differences, like saying 'please', we're now going to cover the word for manners, or we would cover the word for manners if there were an exact Greek word for it! We know what you must be thinking. The Greek word which is used to mean manners is ΤΡΟΠΟΙ (tropi) = manners, method, or way. Instantly, by the definition, you notice that it is not an exact equivalent. You are right. To narrow down the meaning a little more, in Greek, you have to say ΤΡΟΠΟΙ ΣΥΜΠΕΡΙΦΟΡΑΣ (tropi siberiforas) = means or manner of behaving. This isn't because Greeks have no manners, on the contrary, it is, simply a point of cultural distinction. In Ancient Greece everyone was expected to behave themselves. Therefore everyone behaved within the social norm, and their means or manner of behaviour – ΤΡΟΠΟΙ ΣΥΜΠΕΡΙΦΟΡΑΣ – were equally acceptable. Those few, however, who absolutely stood out from the pack by their truly polished politeness and good manners were considered to be ΕΥΓΕΝΟΙΣ (evyenis) meaning noble. Because of this, the word also became synonymous with good and better behaved and those who were noble were said to be possessed of a certain ennobling quality, called ΕΥΓΕΝΕΙΑ (evyenia) = literally meaning nobility. Hence, today someone who is polite is said to possess ΕΥΓΕΝΕΙΑ (evyenia), and to, therefore, be ΕΥΓΕΝΙΚΟΣ (evyenikos) = polite!

Apart from the fact that the word has lent itself to English in words like eulogy and eugenics it also gives us the opportunity to explore one more letter combination: **EY**. The two letters together either make the sound *ev* (as in evolution) or *ef* (as in left) depending on what other letter follows in the word.

Other Greek words which use the **EY** combination are:

ΕΥΧΑΡΙΣΤΩ (efharisto) = thank you

ΕΥΚΟΛΟ (efkolo) = easy

ΔΕΥΤΕΡΑ (theftera) = Monday

One more thing we must mention here is the use of **OI**. This is the last *i* you will have to learn in Greek and to all intents and purposes it should be treated as just an ordinary *i* as in king.

Exercise 5

Mike's problems are far from over yet. As this is Lisa's first visit to his apartment he wants to impress her. He has found out that she is a vegetarian. Deciding to play it safe he is going to make an omelette. He knows roughly what he will put in it and he has a list in English, but after only a week in Greece his Greek is still not good enough to do the shopping. See if you can help him by matching the ingredients on his list with the Greek produce.

ΑΥΓΑ	av-wha	bread
ΓΑΛΑ	wh-ala	tomatoes
ΛΑΔΙ	lathi	cheese
ΤΥΡΙ	tiri	salt
ΒΟΥΤΗΡΟ	vootiro	eggs
ΨΩΜΙ	psomi	oil
ΑΛΑΤΙ	alati	butter
ΠΙΠΕΡΙ	piperi	milk
ΝΤΟΜΑΤΕΣ	domates	pepper

> **PIT STOP!**
>
> One of the most common complaints tourists have about Greek food is the temperature it is served at. Hot food, when it comes, has a rather tepid temperature. The reason for this is that Greece is a hot country and food is traditionally served lukewarm or tepid rather than hot. This is a minor cultural difference, but, if you like your food served piping hot, it is an important one.

NOTE: Just as the Greek letters ΜΠ gave us the English B sound, ΝΤ gives us the sound D. We will get a chance to practise this combination in the next couple of chapters.

Letter combinations

To make an omelette ΟΜΕΛΕΤΑ (omeleta), naturally, you need to break some eggs and in order to do so, you must first be able to say the word so you can buy them.

Eggs is one of those funny words in Greek which depends upon a letter combination. This time it is: **ΑΥ** (pronounced *av* as in c**av**ern).

Depending upon which letter comes after it **ΑΥ** can sometimes make the sound *af* (just like in **af**ter) rather than *av* but we'll cover these as and when we get to them.

Exercise 6

Travel does not always broaden the mind. Sometimes it just helps to confuse one nation's flag with another. In the exercise below there are the flags of six nations. The country each represents has, however, been written in Greek. See if you can match them with their English equivalent from the list below.

ΑΜΕΡΙΚΗ   ΙΤΑΛΙΑ   ΕΛΛΑΔΑ   ΙΑΠΩΝΙΑ   ΚΟΡΕΑ
ΑΥΣΤΡΑΛΙΑ

Italy   Korea   Greece   Japan   America   Australia

Lisa's visit to Mike's holiday apartment has gone like a dream. The omelette he made was edible, the Greek salad he prepared was good and they both had a few drinks. As a matter of fact they are so excited by the discovery that this is the other's first trip abroad that they have decided to meet the following day to tackle the lower case letters of the Greek alphabet together. We shall, of course, join them!

YOU'VE JUST LEARNT

AY	– *av* or *af*	**OI**	– *i*
EY	– *ev* or *ef*	**NT**	– *d*

Solutions

Exercise 1

Bread	ΨΩΜΙ
Cheese	ΤΥΡΙ
Beer	ΜΠΥΡΑ
Coffee	ΚΑΦΕΣ
Sugar	ΖΑΧΑΡΗ
Retsina	ΡΕΤΣΙΝΑ
Milk	ΓΑΛΑ
Oil (to cook with)	ΛΑΔΙ
Whisky	ΟΥΙΣΚΙ
Orangeade	ΠΟΡΤΟΚΑΛΑΔΑ

Exercise 2

ΣΟΥΠΕΡΜΑΡΚΕΤ	ΤΥΡΟΠΩΛΕΙΟ	ΓΑΛΑΚΤΟΠΩΛΕΙΟ
ΠΟΡΤΟΚΑΛΑΔΑ	ΤΥΡΙ	ΓΑΛΑ
ΛΑΔΙ		
ΖΑΧΑΡΗ		
ΟΥΙΣΚΙ		
ΚΑΦΕΣ		
ΜΠΥΡΑ		
ΡΕΤΣΙΝΑ		
ΨΩΜΙ		

Exercise 3

1 ΚΑΦΕΣ	ΟΥΖΕΡΙ
2 ΠΟΡΤΟΚΑΛΑΔΑ	
3 ΜΕΖΕΣ	ΤΑΒΕΡΝΑ
4 ΟΥΖΟ	
5 ΚΡΑΣΙ	ΚΑΦΕΤΕΡΙΑ
6 ΜΠΥΡΑ	
7 ΠΙΤΣΑ	
8 ΠΑΤΑΤΕΣ	ΜΠΥΡΑΡΙΑ
9 ΣΑΓΑΝΑΚΙ	
10 ΚΕΦΤΕΔΑΚΙΑ	ΠΙΤΣΑΡΙΑ

Exercise 4

			Κ	Ρ	Α	Σ	Ι
			Ν	Ε	Ρ	Ο	
	Μ	Α	Ρ	Τ	Ι	Ν	Ι
	Ο	Υ	Ι	Σ	Κ	Ι	
	Τ	Ε	Κ	Ι	Λ	Α	
Λ	Ε	Μ	Ο	Ν	Α	Δ	Α
			Γ	Α	Λ	Α	

Exercise 5

ΑΥΓΑ	av-wh**a**	eggs
ΓΑΛΑ	wh-**a**la	milk
ΛΑΔΙ	l**a**thi	oil
ΤΥΡΙ	tir**i**	cheese
ΒΟΥΤΗΡΟ	v**oo**tiro	butter
ΨΩΜΙ	psom**i**	bread

ΑΛΑΤΙ	alati	salt
ΠΙΠΕΡΙ	piperi	pepper
ΝΤΟΜΑΤΕΣ	domates	tomatoes

Exercise 6

| ΑΜΕΡΙΚΗ | ΙΤΑΛΙΑ | ΕΛΛΑΔΑ | ΙΑΠΩΝΙΑ | ΚΟΡΕΑ | ΑΥΣΤΡΑΛΙΑ |
| America | Italy | Greece | Japan | Korea | Australia |

ΓΛΩΣΣΑΡΙΟ
GLOSSARY

This is the end of Unit five. Technically speaking you're half way through the book and you already know all the capital letters of the Greek alphabet, so this is a good place to have a glossary with all the words you have learnt so far in the order they appear in each unit.

Glossary, is a Greek word of course, and it comes from the word ΓΛΩΣΣΑ (glossa) = tongue. In Greek it also means 'language'. To the ancient Greek mind, language and tongue were so closely connected that they were indistinguishable, and this is something which is reflected in modern Greek today, as there is no other word for language apart from the word ΓΛΩΣΣΑ. For a long time ancient Greek learning and thought influenced Renaissance philosophers who pondered on the phenomenon of language and the fact that different people spoke a different tongue (so to speak). The influence this had on us today is reflected in the survival of such phrases as "mother tongue" and even, "speaking in tongues".

In the glossary which follows we give you the meaning of each word as a handy reference guide and also, where appropriate, its context as well as the capital letter it introduced. Our hope is that each word widens your window into the Greek culture just as it enriches your knowledge of the Greek language.

Unit 1

ΤΑΞΙ – Ξ   taxi. Greek taxis work in taxi ranks but they also cruise the cities and towns as they can stop and pick up passengers anywhere, provided of course the 'taxi' sign on top of the cab is lit.

MINI – M   mini. Literally, the British cult car, but also a short skirt. The mini skirt became popular in Greece in the 60s and 70s along with the car. The latter was particularly suitable for driving through the narrow streets of Greek cities and towns and caused few problems in parking.

MONO – N   alone or only

NOTA – T   a musical note

MAΞI – I   a long skirt. The opposite of a mini skirt.

Unit 2

ΠΑΝΩ – Ω   up. In fact, ΠΑΝΩ is a popular contraction of the word ΕΠΑΝΩ. Many modern Greek words have dropped letters which are not pronounced any more because of popular usage.

ΚΑΤΩ – Ω   down

ΚΑΖΑΝΙ – Z   cauldron. Originally black cauldrons were used in Greek villages to do all the boiling in. This meant that they were used both for cooking food and doing the family laundry (which tended to be mainly grey and black colours). This is a practice which is encountered very rarely these days and then only in the poorest of villages, though the traditional black garb of the mountain villager and the islander still remains popular, particularly in the older quarters of island towns and villages.

ΚΟΜΜΑ – K   comma

ΚΑΚΟ – O   bad. This Greek word has become absorbed into English as a prefix to words such as cacophony (itself a Greek compound word).

ΚΑΛΕΝΑ – Δ   neck or watch chain, usually made of gold.

ΚΑΝΩ – K   I do/I make and I'm doing/I'm making

ΕΛΩ – Ω   here

ΔΥΟ – Y   two. Ancient Greeks were very interested in the concept of 'two' because they firmly believed that everything in the world existed in pairs. They saw good coexisting with bad, hot with cold and war with peace. This duality influenced western thought significantly and shaped our philosophies and even our political practices and theological beliefs for over 3,000 years.

ΔΕΞΙΑ – Δ   right (as in direction). Words such as 'dexterity', 'dextrous' and even 'ambidextrous' bear witness to the fact that society has traditionally approved of right handedness.

ΔΕΜΑ – Δ   parcel or packet

ΔΕΚΑ – Δ   the number ten

ΔΕΝ – Δ   not

ΠΟΤΟ – Π   drink. Alcohol in Greece is sold practically everywhere. There are no licensing laws restricting its sale and you can buy beer at two in the morning from your local deli, provided it's still open.

ΠΙΝΩ – Π   I drink, I'm drinking

ΠΑΩ – Π   I go, I'm going

ΠΑΚΕΤΟ – Π   packet or parcel

ΕΝΑ – Ε   one

ΕΞΙ – Ξ   six. A two-dimensional shape with six sides is a hexagon.

ΕΠΤΑ – Π   seven. Depending on where you go, you may hear the number seven pronounced as ΕΦΤΑ or ΕΠΤΑ. The variation in pronunciation may have been regional to start with, although it most probably occurred during the four hundred years when Greece was part of the Ottoman Empire. Greek schools were closed down, and the task of keeping the Greek language alive was then left predominantly to the church, which was successful, despite the threat of the death penalty if discovered. This variation occurs in a few other words which we'll encounter. There is no cultural stigma attached to either and both are equally well understood.

ΟΚΤΩ – Ω   eight. Again this may be pronounced as either ΟΚΤΩ or ΟΧΤΩ.

ΕΝΝΕΑ – Ε   nine. Sometimes pronounced ΕΝΝΙΑ.

ΔΕΚΑ – Δ   ten. In English we find it in such 'borrowed' words as decalogue.

ΔΩΔΕΚΑ – Δ   twelve. A dodecahedron, in geometry, is a three dimensional twelve-sided object.

ΔΕΚΑΕΞΙ – Δ   sixteen

ΔΕΚΑΕΠΤΑ – Δ   seventeen. Again this one may be pronounced ΔΕΚΑΕΠΤΑ or ΔΕΚΑΕΦΤΑ.

ΔΕΚΑΟΚΤΩ – Ω   eighteen. Pronounced either ΔΕΚΑΟΚΤΩ or ΔΕΚΑΟΧΤΩ.

ΤΟΞΟ – Ξ   bow, as used in archery. 'Toxic' derives from the classical Greek word for arrow poison.

ΙΔΕΑ – A   idea. The ancient Greeks believed that ideas had an existence outside the world of the mind. They believed that, once grasped, they revealed something about the world which existed in the metaphysical realm. This provided Greek thinkers of the time with the ability to visualise and carry out complex thought experiments using no aid other than that of rigorous logic. While this helped them make some truly astounding discoveries, like the concept of atoms for example, it also hampered the appearance of the experimental method for a great many centuries.

ΑΤΟΜΟ – A   atom and individual. It was Democritus the Abderite (also known as the Laughing Philosopher, for his pleasant, easy-going approach to life) who first came up with the theory of atoms making up the world. Carrying out a thought experiment, Democritus visualised cutting things down into smaller pieces until he arrived at the concept of a spherical body so tiny that it could no longer be cut. The ancient Greek word for cut was ΤΟΜΗ and the prefix A- in front meant 'not'. Therefore ΑΤΟΜΟ was something which literally could not be cut any further, or at least not without destroying its distinct identity, pretty much like individuals!

Unit 3

ΕΝΑ – N   the number 1

ΚΑΦΕ – Φ   coffee and the colour brown.

ΣΗΜΑ – H   sign and badge. It also means signal.

ΣΟΚ – Σ   shock. This is an imported word into Greek.

ΣΟΦΙΑ – Φ   wisdom. In ancient Greece there was an Olympian goddess called Wisdom and she was the one responsible for those who were, indeed, wise.

ΛΑΟΣ – Λ   people massed together, and race as in a race of people.

ΛΑΔΙ – Λ   oil

ΕΛΕΟΣ – Λ   mercy. This is a word connected to the Greek word for oil, ΛΑΔΙ, because an olive wreath was given as a token of peace between the Greek city-states (at the end of an armed conflict).

ΠΟΛΥ – Λ   very, a lot

ΕΛΛΗΝΙΚΟΣ – Λ   Greek. It is also the name by which Greek coffee, a potent brew, is known. It used to be known as Turkish coffee (ΤΟΥΡΚΙΚΟΣ) until the early 1970s when relations between Turkey and Greece deteriorated. It was decided then that it should be known as Greek coffee, though quite a few people still persist in ordering it as Turkish coffee at their local coffee shop.

ΓΛΥΚΟ – Γ   sweet

ΓΑΛΑ – Γ   milk

ΓΙΑΤΙ – Γ   why, because. It is not unusual in Greek to answer a question beginning with ΓΙΑΤΙ with a sentence also beginning with ΓΙΑΤΙ.

ΓΙΑ – Γ   for

ΚΑΦΕΔΕΣ – Φ   coffees

ΝΕΡΟ – Ρ   water. In Greece, coffee is traditonally always accompanied with a glass of water.

ΝΕΡΑ – Ρ   funnily enough, the plural of water (whether it is a glass of water or water in general) is waters!

ΠΑΡΑΚΑΛΩ – Ω   please. In Greek, 'please' comes from a word which originally meant 'I beg'. Therefore, translated literally, ΠΑΡΑΚΑΛΩ means, 'I beg of you'.

ΑΓΟΡΑ – Ρ   a market

ΑΓΟΡΑΖΩ – Ρ   I buy, I'm buying

ΟΥΖΟ – ΟΥ   ouzo, the fiery Greek drink.

ΟΥΖΕΡΙ –   a specialist outlet, traditionally cheap, where sailors and villagers would congregate to drink ouzo and listen to live music played on a mandolin.

ΚΡΑΣΙ – Σ   wine

ΤΕΚΙΛΑ – Λ   tequila

ΟΥΙΣΚΙ – ΟΥ   whisky

ΜΑΡΤΙΝΙ – P   martini

ΛΕΜΟΝΑΔΑ – Δ   lemonade

ΠΟΡΤΟΚΑΛΑΔΑ – Π   orangeade

ΜΕΖΕΣ – Ζ   tit bit. The concept of ΜΕΖΕΣ was born out of necessity. In earlier times when refrigeration was a problem, eating places which served wine and ouzo were faced with the dilemma of what to serve with it. A ΜΕΖΕΣ can be anything from fried cheese to chips or meatballs.

ΣΑΓΑΝΑΚΙ – Γ   traditional ouzeri food. It consists of fried hard cheese and fried squid or octopus served in a light vinaigrette dressing.

ΟΚΤΑΠΟΔΙ – Δ   It literally means eight-legged and is, of course, the octopus.

ΚΕΦΤΕΔΑΚΙΑ – Φ   small meatballs

ΠΑΤΑΤΕΣ – Π   potatoes and also chips!

ΛΕΩΦΟΡΕΙΟ – ΕΙ   bus

ΘΕΛΩ – Θ   I want

ΘΕΛΕΙΣ – Θ   you want

ΘΕΛΕΙ – Θ   he/she/it wants

ΘΕΛΟΥΜΕ – Θ   we want

ΘΕΛΕΤΕ – Θ   you want

ΘΕΛΟΥΝΕ – Θ   they want

ΚΑΙ – ΑΙ   and

ΜΕ – Μ   with

ΜΠΑΡ – ΜΠ   bar. This is another one of those imported words. As modern Greek uses a combination of letters in order to reproduce the sound *B*, it makes for some very funny looks from English speakers when it's encountered on signs.

ΜΠΟΥΚΑΛΙ – ΜΠ   bottle

ΜΠΥΡΑ – ΜΠ   beer. Quite a lot of beer is drunk in Greece.

ΜΠΟΥΚΑΛΙΑ – ΜΠ   bottles

ΠΙΤΣΑ – ΤΣ   pizza

ΠΙΤΣΑΡΙΑ – ΤΣ   the place where you would expect to buy a pizza.

ΚΑΦΕΤΕΡΙΑ – Φ   a coffee shop. Greek coffee shops tend to be very popular places and quite a lot of them will also do food like pizza and barbecued chicken with chips.

ΜΠΥΡΑΡΙΑ – ΜΠ   where you would go to drink beer and have a meze.

ΤΑΒΕΡΝΑ – Β   Traditionally Greek tavernas served mainly wine, usually a number of local varieties straight from the barrel, as well as the Greek retsina.

ΒΙΒΛΙΟ – Β   book

ΒΑΖΟ – Β   vase

ΒΟΥΤΗΡΟ – ΟΥ   butter

ΔΡΑΧΜΗ – Χ   the Greek currency.

ΕΚΑΤΟ – Ο   a hundred

Unit 4

ΧΙΛΙΑ – Χ   a thousand. ΧΙΛΙΑ has loaned itself, in a slightly altered form, into words such as kilometre (a thousand metres) and kilogram (a thousand grams).

ΨΑΡΙ – Ψ   fish

ΨΩΜΙ – Ψ   bread. In many places, Greek bread is still made in a stone-floored oven.

ΨΩΝΙΖΩ – Ψ   I buy and I am buying.

ΦΡΟΥΤΟΠΩΛΕΙΟ – ΕΙ   a place where you would go to buy fresh produce. In Greece, for many years, such shops provided the only outlet available to local farmers. In many places they still do.

ΦΡΟΥΤΑ – ΟΥ   fruit

ΤΥΡΟΠΩΛΕΙΟ – ΕΙ   a shop specialising in the sale of cheese. Cheese was usually kept in wooden caskets, in brine, to preserve it and you used to be able to try it before you bought it. Progress in the form of air-tight, sealed packaging is doing away with the few cheese shops which are left.

ΤΥΡΙ – Υ   cheese

ΓΑΛΑΚΤΟΠΩΛΕΙΟ – ΕΙ   a shop selling only dairy produce such as eggs, milk and yoghurt. It would normally be run by the local milkman who would also have a delivery round in the area. Until the early 1970s the round would consist of a milk delivery in the morning and another delivery for yoghurt and eggs in the early evening. The milk is goat or sheep milk, and the yoghurt would have been made during the day by the milkman, hence the second delivery. Similarly, hens' eggs would have been laid and collected that day!

ΨΑΡΟΠΩΛΕΙΟ – Ψ   a fishmonger's. They were normally run by fishermen who would use them to sell their catch of the day.

Unit 5

ΩΡΑ – Ω   time. This word has become the basis for borrowed English words such as horoscope (which depends upon an accurate knowledge of one's time of birth in order to cast) and horology (the art of clockmaking).

ΨΩΝΙΑ – Ω   the shopping, i.e. things you have bought.

ΜΑΓΑΖΙ – Γ   shop. This is applied in a generic manner to any shop in Greece.

ΖΑΧΑΡΗ – Χ   sugar

ΡΕΤΣΙΝΑ – ΤΣ   the famous Greek wine, which takes its name from the resin now used to flavour it. It's believed that originally it came about when either wood resin from wine barrels which had not been properly cured or resin used to seal them, got into the wine by accident.

ΤΡΟΠΟΙ – ΟΙ   manners, method, way

ΣΥΜΠΕΡΙΦΟΡΑ – ΜΠ   behaviour

ΤΡΟΠΟΙ ΣΥΜΠΕΡΙΦΟΡΑΣ –   manners, literally way of behaviour

ΕΥΓΕΝΗΣ – ΕΥ   noble, polite

ΕΥΓΕΝΕΙΑ – ΕΙ   politeness, also, quite literally, nobility.

ΕΥΓΕΝΙΚΟΣ – ΕΥ   polite

ΕΥΧΑΡΙΣΤΩ – ΕΥ   thank you

A B Γ Δ E Z H Θ I K Λ M N Ξ O Π P Σ T Y Φ X Ψ Ω

ΕΥΚΟΛΟ – ΕΥ   easy

ΔΕΥΤΕΡΑ – ΕΥ   Monday. In Greek it literally means the second day of the week.

ΑΥΓΑ – ΑΥ   eggs

ΑΛΑΤΙ – Λ   salt

ΠΙΠΕΡΙ – Π   pepper

ΝΤΟΜΑΤΕΣ – ΝΤ   tomatoes

ΟΜΕΛΛΕΤΑ – Λ   omelette. This is one of those words, which though borrowed is now considered 'Greek' and follows the grammar of the Greek language.

ΑΜΕΡΙΚΗ – Η   America

ΙΤΑΛΙΑ – Ι   Italy

ΕΛΛΑΔΑ – Λ   Greece

ΙΑΠΩΝΙΑ – Π   Japan

ΚΟΡΕΑ – Ρ   Korea

ΑΥΣΤΡΑΛΙΑ – ΑΥ   Australia

6 | ΨΩΝΙΑ!
SHOPPING!

Well, here we are, with all the capitals of the alphabet completed and about to rush into the world of the lower case letters. These will be easier because there are stress marks to help you pronounce the words. As before, there's good news ☺ and there's ... even better news. ☺☺ The good news is that Greek does not have joined-up writing, therefore the letters you'll learn stay pretty much the same when they're written. The even better news is that many letters remain the same as they were in their capital form. They're just written smaller! This explains why capitals and lower case letters are usually referred to in Greek as Big and Small letters. ΜΕΓΑΛΑ (mewhala) and ΜΙΚΡΑ (mikra).

Exercise 1

In our first exercise however we will take a look at the 'Big' letters by trying to match the names of some of the silver screen's biggest fictional detectives with their Greek equivalents. Draw a line connecting the correct answers and practise saying the Greek names aloud:

POIROT	ΣΕΡΛΟΚ ΧΟΛΜΣ
SHERLOCK HOLMES	ΠΟΥΑΡΟ
PHILIP MARLOW	ΕΠΙΘΕΩΡΗΤΗΣ ΜΟΡΣ
ELLIOT NES	ΜΑΓΝΟΥΜ
MAGNUM	ΦΙΛΙΠΠΟΣ ΜΑΡΛΟΟΥ
INSPECTOR MORSE	ΕΛΙΟΤ ΝΕΣ

Sleuths

We promised you some practice with the combination of Greek letters which give us the sound *D* and we're just about to deliver. All of the above fictional personalities, to a greater or lesser extent are detectives. The Greek word for detective has been taken directly from the English and it's used to mean both a detective (as in the police rank) and a private investigator.

Below we give you the word in capitals. First practise saying it ALOUD a few times, just so you can get your tongue round it. Next, see if you can rewrite it in the space provided using only lower case letters. Check at the top of the page if you are not sure.

ΝΤΕΝΤΕΚΤΙΒ

- - - - - - - - - -

It's a 'D' thing

Now that you're good, see if you can match the Greek names on the left with the English ones on the right.

Ντόναλντ Ντάκ	Davy Crocket
ΝΤΕΙΒΙΝΤ ΚΡΟΚΕΤ	Diana Ross
ΝΤΑΙΑΝΑ ΡΟΣ	Danny de Vito
Ντάνι ντε Βίτο	Donald Duck

First impressions

Mike has a problem. He likes Lisa and would like to impress her even more. After she left his apartment he stayed up half the night going through his language guide books trying to learn the names of the places he would like to take her to. What he has discovered is that a lot of the signs in shops are in lower case letters and these look very different from their capital counterparts! See if you can help him by matching the capitals with their lower case letters in the list opposite.

ΠΙΤΣΑΡΙΑ	Ουζερί
ΟΥΖΕΡΙ	Μπυραρία
ΚΑΦΕΤΕΡΙΑ	Πιτσαρία
ΜΠΥΡΑΡΙΑ	Καφετερία

Here's one you'd never guess

Because of its Ancient Greek roots, modern Greek positively bristles with words loaded with poetic imagery. Take the one below for example:

ΟΠΩΡΟΠΩΛΕΙΟ (oporopolio) = fruit shop

The basis of this one comes from the word ΟΠΩΡΑ (opora) meaning produce from trees, which originally would have been the only kind of fresh produce available to buy. While no one calls it ΟΠΩΡΟΠΩΛΕΙΟ any more, the signs outside fruit shops still serve as a reminder of days when greenhouses and international trade did not exist.

See if you can now substitute lower case letters for each upper one of the word:

ΟΠΩΡΟΠΩΛΕΙΟ

The lower case letters

Although you've already met some lower case letters and now know just how easy it is to leap from the capitals to them, it might help if, at this stage, we started from the very beginning:

A α – **alpha**

B β – v**i**ta

Γ γ – **ga**mma

Δ δ – **the**lta

E ε – **e**psilon

Z ζ – **z**ita

H η – **i**ta

Θ θ – **thi**ta

Next to each of these we have included the handwritten version which is different for some. The reason handwriting is slightly different from what you will see on shop signs and windows has more to do with the human personality than grammar, so it's sufficient to say that it differs and leave it at that. Now that you're ready we'll tackle the rest of the lower case letters:

I ι – yota _____ ι

K κ – kappa _____ κ

Λ λ – lamda _____ λ

M μ – mi _____ ʮ

N ν – ni _____ ν

Ξ ξ – ksi _____ ξ

O o – omikron _____ o

Π π – pi _____ π

P ρ – rho _____ ρ

Σ σ – sigma _____ ϛ

T τ – taf _____ τ

Y υ – ipsilon _____ υ

Φ φ – fi _____ φ

X χ – hee _____ χ

Ψ ψ – psi _____ ψ

Ω ω – omega _____ ω

In other words

Mike is finding himself getting in deeper and deeper problems. As he looks at all the places he wants to take Lisa to, he realises that some of these he can understand but some others do not seem to bear much resemblance to anything else. See if you can help him untangle the mess he is in by matching the place with its English definition and what it sells or what services it provides! To help you in the task we have provided a glossary at the end of this unit. To make things harder though ☺☺ we used only lower case letters. See how you do. Use the top of the page to guide you.

ΧΡΥΣΟΧΟΕΙΟ	Bakery	ΚΑΦΕ
ΞΕΝΟΔΟΧΕΙΟ	Hotel	ΦΙΛΜ
ΑΡΤΟΠΩΛΕΙΟ	Jeweller's	ΧΟΡΟΣ
ΖΑΧΑΡΟΠΛΑΣΤΕΙΟ	Café	ΦΑΓΗΤΟ
ΚΑΦΕΤΕΡΙΑ	Cinema	ΨΩΜΙ
ΕΣΤΙΑΤΟΡΕΙΟ	Restaurant	ΧΡΥΣΟΣ
ΚΙΝΗΜΑΤΟΓΡΑΦΟΣ	Patisserie	ΓΛΥΚΑ
ΝΤΙΣΚΟΤΕΚ	Disco	ΔΩΜΑΤΙΟ
ΦΑΡΜΑΚΕΙΟ	Chemist	ΑΣΠΙΡΙΝΗ
ΤΑΧΥΔΡΟΜΕΙΟ	Post Office	ΓΡΑΜΜΑΤΟΣΗΜΑ

Exercise 2

Look at the cut-outs of some of the Greek newspapers. First say the name of each newspaper aloud. Then, in the space provided, replace the capitals with the lower case letters:

ΑΠΟΓΕΥΜΑΤΗΝΗ, ΑΚΡΟΠΟΛΗ, ΜΕΣΗΜΕΡΙΑΝΗ,

_____ _____ _____

ΚΥΡΗΚΑΣ, ΕΘΝΙΚΗ,   ΠΕΛΟΠΟΝΝΗΣΟΣ

_____ _____   _____

How did you do?

Check your answers at the end of the chapter and if you've scored less than 5/6 look at the capitals and lower case letters again! Circle the ones which you've got wrong and practise writing them a few times. Recognition comes only with repetition!

How much?

In the exercise below you need to identify which price tag belongs to which group of words. Unfortunately they are all jumbled up and the words are in lower case letters!

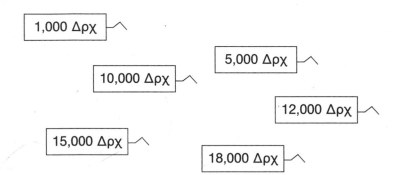

χίλιες δραχμές, δεκαοκτώ χιλιάδες δραχμές, δώδεκα χιλιάδες δραχμές, πέντε χιλιάδες δραχμές, δέκα χιλιάδες δραχμές, δεκαπέντε χιλιάδες δραχμές.

One extra letter

The number of lower case letters in the Greek alphabet is, funnily enough, one more than the capitals! This is because of the letter Σ (sigma). In its capital form, sigma presents no problem, but when we go to the lower case letter, a small problem becomes apparent. A different form of sigma is needed at the beginning and in the middle of a word to the

---

⌘ PIT STOP!

Many of the words we use in the English language have been passed on to us by the Greeks, though we don't necessarily use them in the same context. The Greek word for newspaper, for example, is EΦHMEPIΔA (efimeritha). This has given rise to the word ephemeral – which is what news is by nature!

one needed at the end. The sigma which is used at the end of a Greek word is, to all intents and purposes, identical to the English -ς. The sigma used at the beginning and in the middle is simply -σ.

So, ΓΛΥΚΟΣ (sweet) which is what you want the coffee you're ordering to be, becomes in lower case γλυκος.

In a long word like locomotive, for example, the letter -s occurs several times.

We give you the word in capitals and ask you to write it in small case letters:

ΣΙΔΗΡΟΔΡΟΜΟΣ (sithirothromos)

Literally speaking

A lot of the modern Greek words came about as exact descriptions of what they are.

ΣΙΔΗΡΟΣ (sithiros) means iron and ΔΡΟΜΟΣ (thromos) means road. So, ΣΙΔΗΡΟΔΡΟΜΟΣ stands for both the railway network (literally, iron road) and the trains which run on it. Of course, the more modern word for train is ΤΡΑΙΝΟ (treno).

In the next exercise Mike and Lisa face a problem. They want to buy a ticket for a ferry crossing. Unfortunately the book they have uses numerals to number the words written in capital letters, lower case Greek letters to number their definitions in English and capital Greek letters to number the words written in lower case Greek letters! Our two friends are totally confused. See if you can help them by matching the number with its equivalent letter in both Greek and English to arrive at the lower case form and definition of the word. One has been done for you as an example:

Example: 12 ΑΕΡΟΠΛΑΝΟ   μ aeroplane   Μ αεροπλάνο

1 ΣΙΔΗΡΟΔΡΟΜΟΣ	α train	Α τρένο
2 ΛΕΟΦΟΡΕΙΟ	ε helicopter	Β λεοφορείο
3 ΑΥΤΟΚΙΝΗΤΟ	δ ferry	Ε ελικόπτερο
4 ΦΕΡΙΜΠΟΤ	ζ coach	Δ φεριμπότ
5 ΕΛΙΚΟΠΤΕΡΟ	θ cable car	Η φορτηγό

6 ΠΟΥΛΜΑΝ	β	bus	Κ	τάνξ
7 ΦΟΡΤΗΓΟ	ι	submarine	Γ	αυτοκίνητο
8 ΤΕΛΕΦΕΡΙΚ	γ	car	Θ	τελεφερίκ
9 ΥΠΟΒΡΥΧΙΟ	κ	tank	Ζ	πούλμαν
10 ΤΑΝΞ	η	truck	Ι	υποβρύχιο
11 ΑΕΡΟΠΛΑΝΟ	λ	taxi	Μ	αεροπλάνο
12 ΤΑΞΙ	μ	aeroplane	Λ	ταξί

Exercise 3

This morning, Mike found that he needed a few odds and ends, so he has spent the last half hour dashing from shop to shop, before meeting up with Lisa at their favourite café. Unfortunately his bag has become mixed up with those of other shoppers. Mike bought something at each of the following shops and also at a fruit and vegetable stall. Can you guess which bag is his?

ΖΑΧΑΡΟΠΛΑΣΤΕΙΟ

ΑΡΤΟΠΩΛΕΙΟ

ΓΑΛΑΚΤΟΠΩΛΕΙΟ

ΒΙΒΛΙΟΠΩΛΕΙΟ

ΤΑΧΥΔΡΟΜΕΙΟ

You have met most of these words before. However, so as not to make it too easy, we have thrown in a few new ones, but you won't have any problems with them.

Bag 1	Bag 2	Bag 3	Bag 4	Bag 5
ψωμί	γάλα	γλυκό	ένα πορτοκάλι	ψωμί
πέντε ντομάτες	μήλα	ψωμί	γραμματόσημα	τυρί
μπουκάλι κρασί	βιβλίο	κρασί	τυρί	ένα γλυκό
φέτα	γραμματόσημα	τυρί	ουίσκι	καρπούζι
γιαούρτι	σοκολάτα	βούτυρο	δύο βιβλία	βούτυρο
τυρί	ψωμί	γάλα	γιαούρτι	γάλα

> **What's new?**
>
> μήλα = apples, γιαούρτι = yoghurt, μπισκότα = biscuits,
> λεμόνια = lemons, σοκολάτα = chocolate, καρπούζι = water melon,
> βούτηρο = butter, πορτοκάλι = orange

Solutions

Exercise 1

POIROT	ΠΟΥΑΡΟ
SHERLOCK HOLMES	ΣΕΡΛΟΚ ΧΟΛΜΣ
PHILIP MARLOW	ΦΙΛΙΠΠΟΣ ΜΑΡΛΟΟΥ
ELLIOT NES	ΕΛΙΟΤ ΝΕΣ
MAGNUM	ΜΑΓΝΟΥΜ
INSPECTOR MORSE	ΕΠΙΘΕΩΡΗΤΗΣ ΜΟΡΣ

First impressions

ΠΙΤΣΑΡΙΑ	Πιτσαρία
ΟΥΖΕΡΙ	Ουζερί
ΚΑΦΕΤΕΡΙΑ	Καφετερία
ΜΠΥΡΑΡΙΑ	Μπυραρία

In other words

ΧΡΥΣΟΧΟΕΙΟ – ΧΡΥΣΟΣ – jeweller's

ΞΕΝΟΔΟΧΕΙΟ – ΔΩΜΑΤΙΟ – hotel

ΑΡΤΟΠΩΛΕΙΟ – ΨΩΜΙ – bakery

ΖΑΧΑΡΟΠΛΑΣΤΕΙΟ – ΓΛΥΚΑ – patisserie

ΚΑΦΕΤΕΡΙΑ – ΚΑΦΕ – cafeteria

ΕΣΤΙΑΤΟΡΕΙΟ – ΦΑΓΗΤΟ – restaurant

ΚΙΝΗΜΑΤΟΓΡΑΦΟΣ – ΦΙΛΜ – cinema

ΝΤΙΣΚΟΤΕΚ – ΧΟΡΟΣ – disco

ΦΑΡΜΑΚΕΙΟ – ΑΣΠΙΡΙΝΗ – chemist

ΤΑΧΥΔΡΟΜΕΙΟ – ΓΡΑΜΜΑΤΟΣΗΜΑ – post office

Exercise 2

ΑΠΟΓΕΥΜΑΤΗΝΗ, ΑΚΡΟΠΟΛΗ, ΜΕΣΗΜΕΡΙΑΝΗ,
απογευματηνή   ακρόπολη   μεσημεριανή

ΚΥΡΗΚΑΣ, ΕΘΝΙΚΗ, ΠΕΛΟΠΟΝΝΗΣΟΣ
κύρηκας   εθνική   πελοπόννησος

How much?

1,000 δρχ = χίλιες δραχμές,

18,000 δρχ = δεκαοκτώ χιλιάδες δραχμές,

12,000 δρχ = δώδεκα χιλιάδες δραχμές,

5,000 δρχ = πέντε χιλιάδες δραχμές,

10,000 δρχ = δέκα χιλιάδες δραχμές,

15,000 δρχ = δεκαπέντε χιλιάδες δραχμές.

Literally speaking

1–α–Α, 2–β–Β, 3–γ–Γ, 4–δ–Δ, 5–ε–Ε, 6–ζ–Ζ, 7–η–Η, 8–θ–Θ, 9–ι–Ι, 10–κ–Κ, 11–λ–Λ, 12–μ–Μ

Exercise 3

It is only **Bag 2** which meets all the criteria.

GLOSSARY

χρυσοχοείο = jeweller's
αρτοπωλείο = bakery
ντισκοτέκ = disco
ταχυδρομείο = post office
φαρμακείο = chemist
κινηματογράφος = cinema
εστιατόρειο = restaurant
ξενοδοχείο = hotel
ζαχαροπλαστείο = patisserie
καφετερία = cafeteria
φαγητό = food
ψωμί = bread
χρυσός = gold
γλυκά = sweets
δωμάτιο = room
φίλμ = movie/film
καφέ = coffee
ασπιρίνη = aspirin
γραμματόσημα = stamps
χορός = dance

7 | ΤΡΩΜΕ ΕΞΩ
EATING OUT

Eating out is a national pastime in Greece. As in most Mediterranean countries people in Greece use eating out as a means of getting together with friends and family. Not surprisingly, prices are cheaper and there is a large variety of restaurants catering to demand.

Below is a menu from one of them. It is written in a combination of lower case and capitals and in English also. The printer was very good at languages but terrible with numbers. He left out half the prices in Greek and half the ones in English. See if you can choose a meal from the list below and then decide how much it will cost you.

MENOY

Γεμιστά	800 δρχ
Πατάτες φούρνου	
Πατάτες τηγανητές	500 δρχ
Παστίτσιο	600 δρχ
Μακαρονάδα Μπολονέζα	1500 δρχ
Μπριζόλα χοιρινή	
Μπριζόλα μοσχαρήσια	1500 δρχ
Κεφτέδες	
Σαλάτα χωριάτικη	
Σαλατα μαρουλι	

MENU

Stuffed tomatoes	
Potatoes cooked in the oven	600 drachs
Chips	
Pastitsio	
Spaghetti Bolognese	
Pork chop	1500 drachs
Beef chop	
Meat balls	800 drachs
Greek salad	500 drachs
Lettuce salad	250 drachs

When are chips not chips?

In Greek the word for potatoes and chips is the same: πατάτες. Potatoes feature quite a lot in Greek cooking. To differentiate between all the different ways of cooking them, Greeks usually describe how they're cooked beside the name. Chips, for example, become πατάτες τηγανητές, literally fried potatoes; while you can also have πατάτες γιαχνή, (steamed potatoes), πατάτες φούρνου (potatoes cooked in the oven), πατάτες βραστές (boiled potatoes) and so on. Because 'fried potatoes' is a long way to say 'chips' Greeks usually call them either πατάτες on its own or πατατάκια (little potatoes) which leaves no doubt whatsoever as to the meaning.

Fast food (Φαστ φουντ)

Greece is not immune to modern day pressures however, and fast food restaurants are popular with young and old alike for the speed and convenience they provide. Over the page we have a number of fast food items you may recognise.

See if you can match the Greek with their English counterparts:

ΧΑΜΠΟΥΡΚΕΡ, ΣΑΝΤΟΥΙΤΣ, ΣΑΛΑΤΑ, ΠΑΤΑΤΕΣ, ΣΩΣ, ΚΕΤΣΑΠ, ΜΟΥΣΤΑΡΔΑ, ΜΠΕΙΚΟΝ

  sauce, salad, mustard, chips, bacon, sandwich, ketchup, hamburger

How did you do? Check at the end of the chapter to see how many you got right.

Now see if you can provide the lower case equivalent for each one.

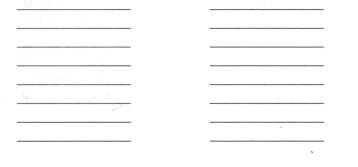

At Goody's

Goody's is a fast food chain in Greece, in the same vein as McDonald's. It aims to provide as healthy a meal as possible. Mike and Lisa decide to try it out. Unfortunately, they've mixed up their translations so they are no longer sure which description fits which choice. See if you can help them by translating the English back into Greek. To help you we have provided some Greek words below.

χάμπουρκερ, σως, υτομάτες, μαρούλι, κρεμμύδι, ψωμάκι, τσιλι, πικολ, μουστάρδα

Translations:
Burger, bread roll, mustard, pickle, sauce

Burger, bread roll, bacon, chilli, sauce, onion, lettuce, tomatoes

Exercise 1

If you have matched the translations correctly you should be able to provide the Greek capitals for the following words:

Bread roll ....
Sauce..
Lettuce...
Bacon...
Tomato...

Exercise 2

Goody's try to provide a lot more than just hamburgers in their menu.
Look at the pictures and descriptions of the choices below.

1

ΚΟΤΟΠΟΥΛΟ GOODY'S

Φιλετάκια από στήθος κοτόπουλου,
τριμμένο καρότο, σως μουστάρδας,
μαρούλι, ντομάτα

2

TEXAS DOUBLE

Ψωμάκι με νιφάδες σταριού, μπιφτέκια,
μπέικον, σως barbeque, τηγανητές
πατάτες, κρεμμύδι, μαρούλι, ντομάτα

3

ΛΟΥΚΑΝΙΚΟ

Λουκάνικο, τηγανητές πατάτες, σως
μουστάρδας, τριμμένο καρότο,
μαρούλι

4

GOODISSIMO ΛΕΥΚΟ

Ζυμαρικό τύπου Linguini, σάλτσα
λευκή, μανιτάρια, μπέικον, τριμμένο
τυρί(παρμεζάνα και σκληρό τυρί)

5

ΜΠΙΦΤΕΚΙ ΜΕ ΤΥΡΙ

Μπιφτέκια, τυρί, σως Goody's,
τηγανητές πατάτες, τριμμένο καρότο

6

GOODISSIMO ΚΟΚΚΙΝΟ

Ζυμαρικό τύπου Linguini, κόκκινη
σάλτσα, τριμμένο τυρί (παρμεζάνα
και σκληρό τυρί)

Now find in which of the choices on the menu the following ingredients appear:

Κοτόπουλο (chicken) ....

Καρότο (carrot) ....

Μπέικον ....

Τυρί ....

Exercise 3

Goody's also do a traditional fish supper! Look at the description below and list all the ingredients in capitals.

Φιλέτα ψαριού, σως tartar, τριμμένο καρότο, τηγανητές πατάτες, αγγούρι, μαρούλι

FISH FILET

> ## PIT STOP!
>
> Greek cuisine, traditionally was dictated to a large extent by the necessities of a mountain-dwelling community. As a result meat does not feature very heavily in it and there are a lot of vegetarian dishes. Because, however, a mountain-dwelling existence is, by definition, harsh, calorie-rich olive oil was used a lot. It continues to play an important role in the Greek diet today, though the rigours of modern Greek life are somewhat less than those of its ancient counterpart.

....
....
....
....
....

Exercise 4

After a hearty meal at Goody's you should treat yourself to an ice cream (ΠΑΓΩΤΟ).

There are three to choose from. Decide which type of ice cream has the ingredients below.

ΠΑΓΩΤΟ GOODY'S

Κρέμα με Cookies, Σοκολάτα με Choc Chips,
Κρέμα με Καραμελωμένα Καρύδια

Κουκις

Caramelised Walnuts

Chocolate

Solutions

Fast food (Φαστ φουντ)

ΧΑΜΠΟΥΡΚΕΡ = hamburger

ΣΑΝΤΟΥΙΤΣ = sandwich

ΣΑΛΑΤΑ = salad

ΠΑΤΑΤΕΣ = chips

ΣΩΣ = sauce

ΚΕΤΣΑΠ = ketchup

ΜΟΥΣΤΑΡΔΑ = mustard
ΜΠΕΙΚΟΝ = bacon

At Goody's

burger	= χάμπουρκερ	burger	= χάμπουρκερ
bread roll	= ψωμάκι	bread roll	= ψωμάκι
mustard	= μουσταρδα	bacon	= μπεικον
pickle	= πίκολ	chilli	= τσίλι
sauce	= σως	sauce	= σως
		onion	= κρεμμύδι
		lettuce	= μαρούλι
		tomatoes	= ντομάτες

Exercise 1

Bread roll = ΨΩΜΑΚΙ   Bacon = ΜΠΕΙΚΟΝ

Sauce = ΣΩΣ   Tomato = ΝΤΟΜΑΤΑ

Lettuce = ΜΑΡΟΥΛΙ

Exercise 2

Κοτόπουλο (chicken)	1
Καρότο (carrot)	1, 3, 5
Μπέικον	2, 4
Τυρί	4, 5, 6

Exercise 3

ΦΙΛΕΤΑ ΨΑΡΙΟΥ
ΣΩΣ TARTAR
ΤΡΙΜΜΕΝΟ ΚΑΡΟΤΟ
ΤΗΓΑΝΗΤΕΣ ΠΑΤΑΤΕΣ
ΑΓΓΟΥΡΙ
ΜΑΡΟΥΛΙ

Exercise 4

Κουκις – Κρέμα με Cookies
Caramelised Walnuts – Κρέμα με καραμελωμένα καρύδια
Chocolate – Σοκολάτα με Choc Chips

You cannot visit Greece without going to at least one museum. Mike and Lisa decided to visit one in Athens. The problem was agreeing on the day to visit it. Lisa thought that Tuesday would be a great day to go but Mike wanted to explore the countryside on a bus on Tuesday. The museum would not be open on the first working day of the week and it would be closed for renovation for the two days prior to Friday, after which it would be open as normal. Mike was suffering from sunburn after the weekend and needed a day to recover and Lisa was adamant that Friday should be set aside for island hopping.

Below are the days of the week in capitals and underneath are spaces for you to write in the lower case letters. Then you need to work out which days of the week are available for Mike and Lisa to go to the museum.

Monday	**Tuesday**	**Wednesday**	**Thursday**
ΔΕΥΤΕΡΑ	ΤΡΙΤΗ	ΤΕΤΑΡΤΗ	ΠΕΜΠΤΗ
_____	_____	_____	_____

Friday	**Saturday**	**Sunday**
ΠΑΡΑΣΚΕΥΗ	ΣΑΒΒΑΤΟ	ΚΥΡΙΑΚΗ
_____	_____	_____

Which days of the week can Mike and Lisa visit the museum? Give the answer in lower case letters _____ _____

Acropolis

The Acropolis is by no means unique to Athens. Every Greek city state had one. Traditionally it was the highest point of the city. It was picked so as to be easily defended and present natural obstacles to any attacker. In the days of ancient Greece the fear of raids from pirates as well as rival city states was very real. If a city state saw itself losing a battle, it would withdraw its army and citizens to the acropolis, surrendering the rest of the city to the invader. Acropolis is a compound word formed from two words, ΑΚΡΗ meaning 'edge' and ΠΟΛΗ meaning 'city'. Acropolis therefore meant literally the edge of the city, or its highest point.

Transportation

In order to make the most of their time in Greece, Mike and Lisa decide to rent some form of transportation. The guidebook they're using however has got wet and some of the letters have faded. They have another guidebook but everything is in lower case letters. The problem is that this guidebook offers no definitions.

Perhaps you can help them by filling in the missing capitals from the words written in lower case.

1 ΣΙ_ΗΡΟ_ _ΟΜΟΣ = train	1 σιδηρόδρομος
2 ΛΕΟΦΟΡ_ _ _ = bus	2 λεοφορείο
3 Α_ _ _ΚΙ_ΗΤΟ = car	3 αυτοκίνητο
4 ΠΟ_ΛΜ_Ν = coach	4 πούλμαν
5 ΦΟΡΤΗ_ _ = truck	5 φορτηγό
6 ΠΟΔΗ_ _ΤΟ = bicycle	6 ποδήλατο
7 Β_ΣΠΑ = scooter	7 βέσπα
8 ΤΖ_Π = Jeep	8 Τζιπ

One more letter combination

There is no single letter which makes the sound *J* in Greek. Again, in order to make that sound Greek has to resort to a combination of letters. In this case they are **T** and **Z**. Together they make exactly the same kind of sound you'd expect to find in **J**ackie, **J**ohn and **J**ames.

Other Greek words which use the letters **TZ** or τζ in their lower case form are:

Τζατζίκι and Τζάζ

Exercise 1

See if you can have a go at this combination by completing the half-written Greek versions of the English names below.

Jake Tod	TZEI_ TO_T
Jasper Carrot	TZA _ _ EP KAPPO_
James Bond	TZEIMΣ MΠO_T
Jill Ireland	_ _ IΛ AIPΛA_ _
James Cooper	_ _ _ _ _ _ KOYΠ_ _
Jackie Onassis	TZA_ _ ONAΣΣH_
John Wayne	TZON Γ_ _ EIN

Home baked apple pie

This is where it gets hard. Very hard. On page 81 is a handwritten recipe for a home-baked apple pie. Look at it carefully and see if you can identify and circle the ingredients from the list below:

Eggs	Αυγα
sugar	ζάχαρη
apples	μήλα
vanilla	βανίλλια
milk	γάλα

Μηλόπιτα

Υλικά:
4 Μήλα (τριμμένα)
2 φρυγανιές τριμμένες
1 κουταλιά ξηρού κανέλλα
1 φλιτζάνι τσαγιού ζάχαρη

1 βιτάμι

2 αυγά

1 ποτήρι νερού γάλα

1 βανίλλια

4 φλιτζάνια τσαγιού αλεύρι

Χτυπάμε τα αυγά με την ζάχαρη
μετά το βιτάμι λιωμένο, την
βανίλλια, το γάλα και το αλεύρι.
Ανακατεύουμε όλα μαζί με
τα τριμμένα μήλα και ψήνουμε
σε προθερμασμένο φούρνο 180°C

Money, money

Below is a list of other countries' currencies in Greek and English. See if you can match the correct ones.

Italian Lira	Αμερικάνικο δολλάριο
Spanish Peseta	Ρώσικο Ρούβλι
Greek Drachma	Ιταλική Λίρα
Russian Rouble	Ισπανική πετσέτα
American Dollar	Ελληνική δραχμή

All capitals

Below is a list of some of the world's capital cities. They're all written in English but the Greek versions are all mixed up between lower and upper case letters and some letters are missing. See if you can fill in the missing letters and then match the Greek words written in capitals with their lower case letter counterpart.

WASHINGTON	ME_IKO	Αθήνα
LONDON	AΘH_ _	Μα_ _ίτη
ATHENS	ΜΑΔΡΙΤΗ	Παρίσ_
MADRID	_ ΑΡΙΣΙ	Ουάσινγκτον
PARIS	ΛΟΝ_Ι_Ο	_εξικό
MEXICO	ΟΥΑΣ_ _ΓΚΤΟ_	_ _νδίνο

Solutions

At the museum

Monday	Tuesday	Wednesday	Thursday
ΔΕΥΤΕΡΑ	ΤΡΙΤΗ	ΤΕΤΑΡΤΗ	ΠΕΜΠΤΗ
Δευτέρα	Τρίτη	Τετάρτη	Πέμπτη

Friday	Saturday	Sunday
ΠΑΡΑΣΚΕΥΗ	ΣΑΒΒΑΤΟ	ΚΥΡΙΑΚΗ
Παρασκευή	Σάββατο	Κυριακή

Days they can go: Σάββατο and Κυριακή

Transportation

1 ΣΙΔΗΡΟΔΡΟΜΟΣ = train	1 σιδηρόδρομος
2 ΛΕΟΦΟΡΕΙΟ = bus	2 λεοφορείο
3 ΑΥΤΟΚΙΝΗΤΟ = car	3 αυτοκίνητο
4 ΠΟΥΛΜΑΝ = coach	4 πούλμαν
5 ΦΟΡΤΗΓΟ = truck	5 φορτηγό
6 ΠΟΔΗΛΑΤΟ = bicycle	6 ποδήλατο
7 ΒΕΣΠΑ = scooter	7 βέσπα
8 ΤΖΙΠ = Jeep	8 Τζίπ

Exercise 1

Jake Tod	ΤΖΕΙΚ ΤΟΝΤ
Jasper Carrot	ΤΖΑΣΠΕΡ ΚΑΡΡΟΤ
James Bond	ΤΖΕΙΜΣ ΜΠΟΝΤ
Jill Ireland	ΤΖΙΛ ΑΙΡΛΑΝΤ
James Cooper	ΤΖΕΙΜΣ ΚΟΥΠΕΡ
Jackie Onassis	ΤΖΑΚΙ ΟΝΑΣΣΗΣ
John Wayne	ΤΖΟΝ ΓΟΥΕΙΝ

Home baked apple pie

Μηλόπιτα

Υλικά:
4 Μήλα (τριμμένα)
2 ψυχανιές τριμμένες
1 κουταλιά Μηλού κανέλλα
1 χυλτζίνι τσαγιού ζάχαρη
1 βιτάκι
2 αυγά
1 ποτήρι νερού λάδι
1 βανίλια
4 χυλτζίνια τσαγιού αλεύρι

Χτυπάμε τα αυγά με την ζάχαρη
μετά το βιτάκι διαλυμένο, την
βανίλια το λάδι και το αλεύρι.
Ανακατεύουμε όλα μαζί με
τα τριμμένα μαζί και μετά σε
σε προθερμανμένο φούρνο 180°C

Money, money

Italian Lira	Ιταλική Λιρα
Spanish Peseta	Ισπανική πετσέτα
Greek Drachma	Ελληνική δραχμή
Russian Rouble	Ρώσικο Ρούβλι
American Dollar	Αμερικάνικο δολλάριο

All capitals

WASHINGTON	ΟΥΑΣΙΝΓΚΤΟΝ	Ουάσινγκτον
LONDON	ΛΟΝΔΙΝΟ	Λονδίνο
ATHENS	ΑΘΗΝΑ	Αθήνα
MADRID	ΜΑΔΡΙΤΗ	Μαδρίτη
PARIS	ΠΑΡΙΣΙ	Παρίσί
MEXICO	ΜΕΞΙΚΟ	Μεξικο

ΤΑΞΙΔΑΚΙΑ
LITTLE TRIPS

Mike and Lisa are really enjoying each other's company. They're enjoying each other's company so much in fact that at the end of a hectic few days' touring they discovered they weren't sure where they went on which days.

Their itinerary was chosen from the list of excursions on offer printed in Greek below. See if you can help them by finding out which package they took. The only clues Mike and Lisa have in their hazy memories are the three sets of tickets they found in their pockets!

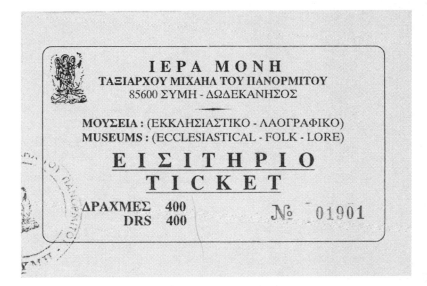

Δελφοί. Η Θόλος στο ιερό της Αθηνάς Προναίας. Αρχές 4ου αι. π.Χ.
Delphi. Tholos in the sanctuary of Athena Pronaia. Beginning of 4th c. BC.

ΑΡΧΑΙΟΛΟΓΙΚΟΣ ΧΩΡΟΣ ΔΕΛΦΩΝ
ARCHAEOLOGICAL SITE OF DELPHI

ΑΧΔ 0 3 5 9 8 2 7

ΕΙΣΙΤΗΡΙΟ
ΕΙΣΟΔΟΥ

ΔΡΧ. 1.200
DRS.

Παρακαλείστε να κρατήσετε το απόκομμα του εισιτηρίου σας
μέχρι την έξοδό σας από το χώρο.
You are requested to preserve your ticket until you leave the Museum/Site

ENTRANCE
T I C K E T

Ημερομ.
7 / ΜΑΙ. 1999

№ 4 1 0 5

ΠΝΕΥΜΑΤΙΚΟ ΙΔΡΥΜΑ ΣΑΜΟΥ

"ΝΙΚΟΛΑΟΣ ΔΗΜΗΤΡΙΟΥ"
ΛΑΟΓΡΑΦΙΚΟ ΜΟΥΣΕΙΟ

ΕΙΣΙΤΗΡΙΟ ΕΙΣΟΔΟΥ
Δρχ. 500
ENTRANCE TICKET

Πυθαγόρειο 83103 Σάμος
Τηλ. (0273) 62286   Fax 62287

ΔΕΥΤΕΡΑ	ΤΡΙΤΗ	ΤΕΤΑΡΤΗ
Ξενοδοχείο	Ξενοδοχείο	Ξενοδοχείο
Δωδεκάνησα	Δελφοί	Δελφοί
Μουσείο – Αθήνα	Σάμος	Σάμος
Ταβέρνα	Εστιατόρειο	Δωδεκάνησα
Ξενοδοχείο	Ξενοδοχείο	Ξενοδοχείο

Exercise 1

This is the part where we give you the opportunity to show us how good you are. We have a word-search exercise below. Find the words listed below and circle them so they join up. When you have done that you should have the outline of four Greek capital letters. When you rearrange them discover what word they spell.

The words which you need to find are:

ψωμί λαός γάλα λάδι ωμέγα σήμα γιατί θέλω
ιδέα αλάτι ψάρι κάνω

Γ	Α	Λ	Α	Β	Γ	Α	Ρ	Ψ	Υ	Λ	Β
Ι	Ρ	Α	Λ	Α	Λ	Μ	Α	Γ	Ω	Ρ	Α
Α	Μ	Π	Α	Ζ	Υ	Ρ	Γ	Ο	Δ	Μ	Τ
Τ	Γ	Ι	Τ	Ο	Ι	Υ	Ρ	Γ	Ι	Α	Ι
Ι	Ψ	Ρ	Ι	Τ	Θ	Ρ	Ι	Τ	Α	Ξ	Κ
Π	Λ	Ο	Υ	Σ	Α	Ε	Ε	Φ	Τ	Α	Δ
Α	Ι	Μ	Π	Α	Ρ	Γ	Λ	Δ	Ν	Υ	Σ
Π	Ο	Τ	Ο	Ψ	Μ	Ν	Ι	Ω	Ω	Μ	Α
Λ	Α	Ο	Σ	Μ	Π	Ι	Ν	Μ	Ρ	Ε	Φ
Α	Ρ	Λ	Η	Μ	Ο	Ν	Ι	Ε	Ε	Ν	Α
Δ	Ε	Ν	Μ	Π	Υ	Ρ	Α	Γ	Κ	Ι	Ν
Ι	Δ	Ε	Α	Κ	Α	Κ	Ο	Α	Α	Μ	Δ

The missing link

Up to now we have covered all the letters of the Greek alphabet and have managed to keep our promise to make them easy and fun. We also did warn you that there was one Greek letter (just one) which caused a few problems.

The gallows shadow of the letter Γ (gamma) takes a little getting used to. We left until now the last combination of letters gamma forms to make the sound *g*.

If the sound appears in the middle of a word, then *G* is formed by ΓΓ.

Example: ENGLAND = ΑΓΓΛΙΑ

If the sound appears at the beginning of a word, then *G* is formed by ΓΚ.

Example: GREY = ΓΚΡΙΖΟ

Other words in Greek where the *g* sound appears are:

ΑΓΓΟΥΡΙ = cucumber

ΑΓΓΕΛΟΣ = angel

ΑΓΓΙΖΩ = I touch

ΑΓΓΛΟΣ = Englishman

Now it's your turn. Write the words above in lower case letters.

_____   _____

_____   _____

The free press

While in Greece, Mike and Lisa spent some time in Athens. Ever ambitious, Mike picked up some newspapers. Look at the front page of Sunday's ΕΛΕΥΘΕΡΟΤΥΠΙΑ.

See if you can circle the Greek words from the list below. We decided to be hard and have given you the list in English. Good luck!

politics, sport, pullover, ten, January's

⅊ PIT STOP!

Greece, the home of democracy, has never really had a 'free' press. Newspapers, traditionally, were strongly affiliated to different political parties. Their readership came from the parties' membership and they were often financed by the party they supported. It is only in recent years that there has been a break from this practice and newspapers are beginning to give a more balanced view of what is happening in Greece.

ΕΚΤΑΚΤΗ ΕΚΔΟΣΗ ΤΗΣ «Κ.Ε.»

31 ΙΑΝΟΥΑΡΙΟΥ 1999 Παρασκευή Β' • Αρ. φύλλου 1.696 • Δρχ. 250

Κυριακάτικη
ΕΛΕΥΘΕΡΟΤΥΠΙΑ
Β' ΕΚΔΟΣΗ

Με μπουφάν και πουλόβερ
ΣΕΛ. 110

Ο «ΚΑΙΡΟΣ» 2, ΠΟΛΙΤΙΚΗ 4, ΠΑΡΑΣΚΗΝΙΑ 18, ΚΟΣΜΟΣ 20, ART 41, ΡΕΠΟΡΤΑΖ 72, ΣΠΟΡ 104

ΕΝΑΣ ΣΤΟΥΣ ΔΕΚΑ πολίτες επενδύουν στο Χρηματιστήριο

ΕΛΛΗΝΙΚΗ ΤΡΕΛΑ ΜΕ ΤΟ ΧΡΗΜΑ

■ Νέο φαινόμενο το «κόμμα των καθικών», αναδιατάσσει την τακτική της κυβέρνησης

Σ ε μια πρωτογνωρη πρωτοπικασία εξέλιξε τα υποελληνικών κοινωνικά έξέλιξη αυτή η οικονομική. Ενας στους 5 ενεργούς πολίτες προεδοκα πόη κερδα απ' το Χρηματιστήριο. Διαμορφώνοντας και μια νέου τύπου πολιτική σημφορορά. Αυτήν ακριβώς μελετούν τώρα τα κόμματα. ΣΕΛ. 4

Τα μυστικά της ασφάλειας
Έκδοση Ιnterland σχίδοση για όλος τις ιδιωτικές ασφαλείας

Πίνακες και χαρτοθεραπεία για διαρκκιαό, αλλά «31 επινδύσεις

ΜΙΑ ΝΕΑ ΣΠΑΝΙΑ ΠΡΟΣΦΟΡΑ

Η ΑΛΛΗ ΟΨΗ ΤΗΣ ΠΑΙΔΕΙΑΣ

Πρώτοι στο μάθημα πρώτοι στον αγώνα
Το παλιό σύνθημα για Άσκημα υπό καταλήψη έχουν «έμπνεε» σα ΑΕΙ
ΣΕΛ. 12

Ο παπα-μπλόκος των καταλήψεων
Αγώνας τους μαθητές, αλλά κάνει τον ...τροχονόμο στην κλείνοντα σ' δρόμο

Island hopping

Mike and Lisa availed themselves of an offer to see as many islands as they could in one day. Below is a map of their journey. They both kept a diary of that day but the good wine and the warm sun did not help their Greek spelling. Perhaps you can help by deciphering exactly where they went that day. Follow their route and then fill in the missing letters from the words below to find out the names of the islands Mike and Lisa visited. Once you have filled in the missing letters re-write the islands in lower case letters.

KPΗTΗ

_____

KAΛOΣ

_____

KAPΠAΘOΣ

_____

XAΛKH

_____

POΔOΣ

_____

ΣΥMH

_____

THΛOΣ

_____

NIΣΥPOΣ

_____

Exercise 2

On their day out to the islands, Mike and Lisa got hungry. Unfortunately, they forgot to take enough money with them. Between them they had 3,000 drachmas. From the menu on pages 92–3 work out what they could have ordered from the restaurant in order to have as balanced a meal as possible.

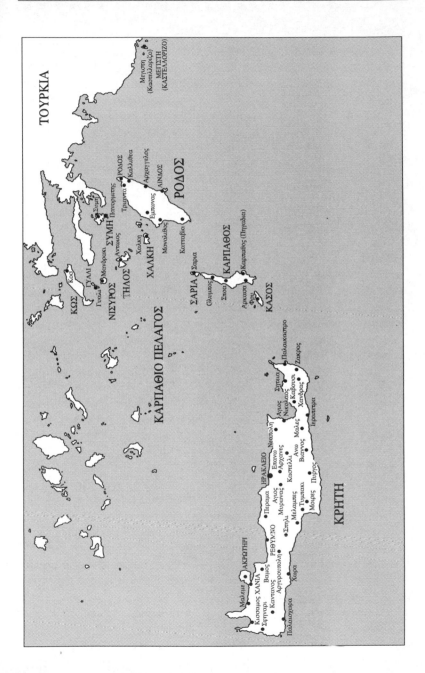

Μπύρες

Gösser ποτήρι 330 ml	500
Gösser ποτήρι 500 ml	700
Heineken	500
Mythos	500
Kaiser	500
Stella Artois	
Amstel	500

Αναψυκτικά

Coca Cola	350
Sprite	350
Πορτοκαλάδα	350
Λεμονάδα	350
Σόδα	350
Μεταλικό νερό	
Εμφιαλωμένο νερό 1 ½ λίτρο	250
Εμφιαλωμένο νερό ½ λίτρο	100
Ούζο (καραφάκι)	700

Κρασί χύμα (το κιλό)	1200

ΚΡΑΣΙΑ

Λευκά

Πελοποννησιακός	2100
Αγιορείτικο	3000
Κτήμα Χατζημιχάλη	3600
Ασπρολίθι	3500
Μαντινεία	3200
Δροσαλίς	2700
Δώρα Διονύσιου	3800
Ροδίτης Αλεπού	2500
Εράσμιος	2800

Ροζέ

Μοναστηριακό	3300
Αλλοτινό	3600
Εσπερίτης	2500

Κόκκινα

Δάφνις	3800
Κατώγι Αβέρωφ	5200
Αμπελοχώρα	3200
Σατυρικό	

Ποτά

Ουίσκυ	1000
Ουίσκυ σπέσιαλ	1400
Βότκα	1000
Τζιν	1000
Μαρτίνι	1000
Campari	1000
Λικέρ	

Ορεκτικά

Πιπεριές γεμιστές	900
Σαγανάκι	700
Μπουρεκάκια	800
Κολοκυθοκεφτέδες	700
Κοτοκροκέτες	900
Κολοκυθόπιτα	1000
Κεφτεδάκια	800
Τυροπιτάκια	600
Πατάτες μερίδα	400
Φέτα	500
Φέτα ψητή	550
Χορτόπιτα	900
Μπουρεκάκια του Σεφ (τυροκροκέτες)	900
Ρυζότο πικάντικο	900
Μανιτάρια α λα κρεμ	1000

Σαλάτες

Σεφ	900
Χωριάτικη	850
Τονοσαλάτα	750
Πατατοσαλάτα	550
Σαλάτα "Επιούσιος„	1000

Κρέπες

Κοτόπουλο	900
Κιμάς, πιπεριά, μανιτάρια	900
Ποικιλία ατομική	1600

Κύριο Πιάτο

Κοτόπουλο "Επιούσιος„	1800
Κοτόπουλο σουβλάκι	1400
Κοτόπουλο φιλέτο	1300
Κοτόπουλο α λα κρεμ	1600
Μπιφτέκι σχάρας	1200
Μπιφτέκι α λα κρεμ	1600
Μπιφτέκι (γεμιστό με τυρί και ζαμπόν)	1500
Μπιφτέκι με ροκφόρ	1500
Σνίτσελ κοτόπουλο	1600
Σνίτσελ χοιρινό	1400
Μπριζόλα χοιρινή	1300
Σουβλάκι χοιρινό (μερίδα)	1400
Λουκάνικο γεμιστό	1200

Ζυμαρικά

Καρμπονάρα	1300
Σεφ	1300
Φούρνου	1200
Πένες 4 τυριά	1300
Μπολονέζ	1100
Ναπολιτέν	900

Solutions

Trips

The only day they could have visited all the places on the tickets is Wednesday.

ΤΕΤΑΡΤΗ

Ξενοδοχείο

Δελφοί

Σάμος

Δωδεκάνησα

Ξενοδοχείο

Exercise 1

Γ	Α	Λ	Α	Β	Γ	Α	Ρ	Ψ	Υ	Λ	Β
Ι	Ρ	Α	Λ	Α	Λ	Μ	Α	Γ	Ω	Ρ	Α
Α	Μ	Π	Α	Ζ	Υ	Ρ	Γ	Ο	Δ	Μ	Τ
Τ	Γ	Ι	Τ	Ο	Ι	Υ	Ρ	Γ	Ι	Α	Ι
Ι	Ψ	Ρ	Ι	Τ	Θ	Ρ	Ι	Τ	Α	Ξ	Κ
Π	Λ	Ο	Υ	Σ	Α	Ε	Ε	Φ	Τ	Α	Δ
Α	Ι	Μ	Π	Α	Ρ	Γ	Λ	Δ	Ν	Υ	Σ
Π	Ο	Τ	Ο	Υ	Μ	Ν	Ι	Ω	Ω	Γ	Α
Λ	Α	Ο	Σ	Μ	Π	Ι	Ν	Μ	Ρ	Ε	Φ
Α	Ρ	Λ	Η	Μ	Ο	Ν	Ι	Ε	Ε	Ν	Α
Δ	Ε	Ν	Μ	Π	Υ	Ρ	Α	Γ	Κ	Ι	Ν
Ι	Δ	Ε	Α	Κ	Α	Κ	Ο	Α	Α	Μ	Δ

The outlined letters are ΠΟΛΥ = very.

The missing link

αγγούρι   άγγελος   αγγίζω   Αγγλος

The free press

Politics = ΠΟΛΙΤΙΚΗ
Sport = ΣΠΟΡ
Pullover = ΠΟΥΛΟΒΕΡ
Ten = ΔΕΚΑ
January's = ΙΑΝΟΥΑΡΙΟΥ

Island hopping

ΚΡΗΤΗ	Κρήτη
ΚΑΣΟΣ	Κάσος
ΚΑΡΠΑΘΟΣ	Καρπάθος
ΧΑΛΚΗ	Χάλκη
ΡΟΔΟΣ	Ρόδος
ΣΥΜΗ	Σύμη
ΤΗΛΟΣ	Τηλός
ΝΙΣΥΡΟΣ	Νίσυρος

Exercise 2

Any combination will do here. It all depends on your own view of what constitutes a balanced meal.

10 | ΣΟΥΒΕΝΙΡ
SOUVENIRS

No matter how good something is, sooner or later, it has to come to an end. This book is no exception. Mike and Lisa, just like you, are now able to recognise practically any combination of Greek letters and pronounce a Greek word, even if they're not too sure about the meaning.

As the days approach for their leaving Greece they begin to look for souvenirs which will remind them of their first wonderful holiday.

The Greek word for souvenir is very easy to recognise: ΣΟΥΒΕΝΙΡ. Now that you know it in capital form, and before we go any further it might be a good idea if you wrote it in lower case letters and decided where the stress should go:

_ _ _ _ _ _ _ _

They all sound the same!

One of the things Mike and Lisa learnt soon after they started to read Greek was that the language has many words which sound nearly identical but have different meanings. The English prefix 'homo' for example comes from the Greek word ΟΜΟΙΟ meaning 'the same/identical'. When added to the word ΦΩΝΗ and suitably altered to sound smoother it becomes ΟΜΟΦΩΝΗ. Homophones, in English, are words with virtually the same pronunciation and different meanings. When it comes to it, though, the Greeks are masters at it. Consider, for example, the following list of ten virtually identical sounding words written in capitals and lower case letters. To find their meaning, all you have to do is identify their numbered counterpart from the box below.

1 χαρτί

2 ΧΑΡΤΗΣ

3 βάζο

4 ΒΑΖΩ

5 κριτής

6 ΚΡΗΤΗ

7 κρίνω

8 ΚΡΙΝΟΣ

9 φύλο

10 ΦΙΛΟΣ

---

10 friend (M) 1 paper 9 sex (M or F) 8 lily 3 vase
6 Crete (the island) 7 I judge 4 I put 2 map 5 judge

Exercise 1

Now reverse the way the ten words are written so that the ones in capital
letters are now written in lower case letters and vice versa.

1 _____

2 _____

3 _____

4 _____

5 _____

6 _____

7 _____

8 _____

9 _____

10 _____

Give them a hand!

If you're having trouble with homophones, spare a little sympathy for the
Greeks themselves. The worst case of a homophone is given to us by the
instance of the word for 'hand' which in very formal Greek (occasionally

referred to by the misnomer of 'High Greek') is χείρα. Unfortunately for the Greeks the word for 'sow' sounds exactly the same although it is spelled χοίρα. (you begin to realise now why there is a need for so many forms of the letter *i*). You will realise just how bad things get when we tell you that the word for widow is also … you guessed it … χήρα!

Now in the days when students from all over Greece had to leave the paternal home and go away to Athens to study at the University there, it would not be unusual to run out of funds very quickly and have to write a hasty, and somewhat pleading, letter home asking for an advance on the following month's allowance. As it was usual, in those days, for the father to handle all family finances it was to him that the letter was addressed and it always finished with the conventional, but somewhat unfortunately chosen, 'I kiss your hand', just before the signature.

Given that there were three possible ways to spell a word which sounds exactly the same, the unfortunate students had a one-in-three chance of getting it right and being bailed out of debt!

Exercise 2

Mike and Lisa have decided to split the souvenirs they buy into three types: ones you can drink, ones you can eat and those you use as mementoes. The problem is that they're now having difficulty remembering any of the Greek words for the things they want to buy. See if you can help them out by completing each list from YOUR OWN memory. Once you have exhausted the words you know you can look at the box at the bottom of this exercise for inspiration. A couple of words will be totally new to you, though by now you're more than adept at figuring them out!

Souvenirs

1 Things you drink	2 Things you eat	3 Mementoes
_____	_____	_____
_____	_____	_____
_____	_____	_____
_____	_____	_____
_____	_____	

_____   _____   _____

_____   _____   _____

_____   _____   _____

> A little help: ούζο, Ελληνικός καφές, άγαλμα, χάρτης, ρετσίνα, φωτογραφία, μπλουζάκι, σημαία, εφημερίδα, γλυκά, βιβλία, εισητήρια, ψώνια, δραχμές, σοκολάτα, Ελληνικό λάδι, πορτοκαλάδα, μπύρα, κασέτα, τσάντα

Greek weather

The weather in Greece is not always as good as tourists seem to think, although sunshine can more or less be guaranteed. The word for 'hot' in Greek is θερμός and from that are derived the words for temperature – θερμοκρασία and thermometer – θερμόμετρο.

On their last day in Greece Mike and Lisa look at a weather report in a local εφημερίδα to decide what to do. Look at the chart on page 100. From the key find the Greek words for the following:

Sunny   _____
Occasional cloud   _____
Heavy cloud   _____
Rain   _____
Thunderstorm   _____
Snow   _____
Fog   _____

From the same weather report write in capitals the names of the large cities, outside Greece, which have a temperature higher than London.

_____   _____

_____   _____

Now write in capitals the names of the Greek towns which have the same temperature as Rome.

_____

_____

Now write the name of the town whose temperature is nearest that of London.

_____

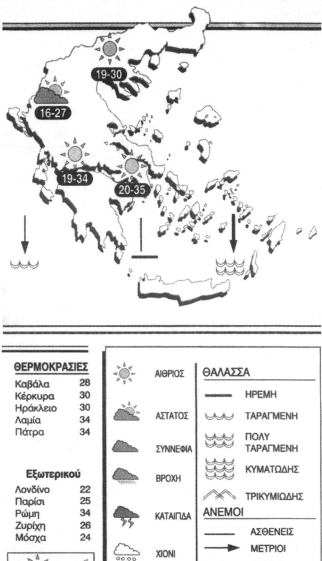

ΘΕΡΜΟΚΡΑΣΙΕΣ

Καβάλα	28
Κέρκυρα	30
Ηράκλειο	30
Λαμία	34
Πάτρα	34

Εξωτερικού

Λονδίνο	22
Παρίσι	25
Ρώμη	34
Ζυρίχη	26
Μόσχα	24

20-36 Κύπρος

ΑΙΘΡΙΟΣ

ΑΣΤΑΤΟΣ

ΣΥΝΝΕΦΙΑ

ΒΡΟΧΗ

ΚΑΤΑΙΓΔΑ

ΧΙΟΝΙ

ΟΜΙΧΛΗ

ΘΑΛΑΣΣΑ

ΗΡΕΜΗ

ΤΑΡΑΓΜΕΝΗ

ΠΟΛΥ ΤΑΡΑΓΜΕΝΗ

ΚΥΜΑΤΩΔΗΣ

ΤΡΙΚΥΜΙΩΔΗΣ

ΑΝΕΜΟΙ

ΑΣΘΕΝΕΙΣ

ΜΕΤΡΙΟΙ

ΙΣΧΥΡΟΙ

ΠΟΛΥ ΙΣΧΥΡΟΙ

ΘΥΕΛΛΩΔΕΙΣ

Acronyms

As the name suggests, acronyms (like acropolis) are quite literally the 'edges of names' or words which, as it happens, are usually defined by their first letters. The Greek word for 'name' is ONOMA and an 'acronym' in Greek is AKPONYMO. By far the most famous (and maybe, initially, the most mystifying) acronym of all time has to be IXΘΥΣ. It is usually found written inside the universal outline of a fish and it has stood for the sign for a Christian for at least the last two thousand years.

Indeed, ιχθύς does mean 'fish'. The reason it also stands for a follower of Christianity is that the letters which coincidentally form the word fish, are themselves an acronym: IHΘOYΣ XPIΣTOΣ, ΘEOYYIOΣ, ΣΩTHP (Jesus Christ, Son of God, Saviour). The acronym becomes even more evident if you rewrite the above sentence in lower case letters but keep the first letter of each word as a capital.

Exercise 3

In their search for souvenirs Mike and Lisa wandered into a shop which sells popular Greek music. They each have 15,000 drachmas and this is the sum total of their money. See if you can help them choose a couple of cassettes each so that they have some money left over for the flight.

More souvenirs

Mike and Lisa also bought a packet of the local Turkish Delight (a remnant of the times when Greece was a principality of the Ottoman empire), although in Greek they naturally call it Greek Delight.

Because Mike is curious he has made a list of all the ingredients used in the making of Greek Delight. Circle the ones you recognise from the list Mike has made and then rewrite them using only capitals.

Ζάχαρη

Νερό

Βανίλλια

Ζελατίνα

Postcards

The Greek word for postcard is καρτ-ποστάλ. Prior to leaving Greece Lisa buys a postcard to leave at her apartment with a thank you on the back. Because she has tried very hard throughout the holiday, Lisa has become quite proficient at writing out lower case Greek. On the back of the postcard she has written:

Το διαμέρισμα
ήταν πολύ ωραίο.

Ευχαριστώ για όλα.

— Λίζα

The flat was very nice.

Thank you for everything.

Lisa

See if you can copy what she has written using only capital letters.

_____   _____

_____

_____

The map

Mike and Lisa's holiday has gone far better than they'd planned. As a matter of fact it's gone so well that they decide to come back next year, together! Mike has gone ahead and bought a map to help them decide where to go. He chose the wrong map however as it only lists a small group of islands, near Turkey! Look at the map on page 104 and then write below, in capital letters, the names of the islands in the order the ferry visits them and then the main city on each island:

_____   _____

_____   _____

_____   _____

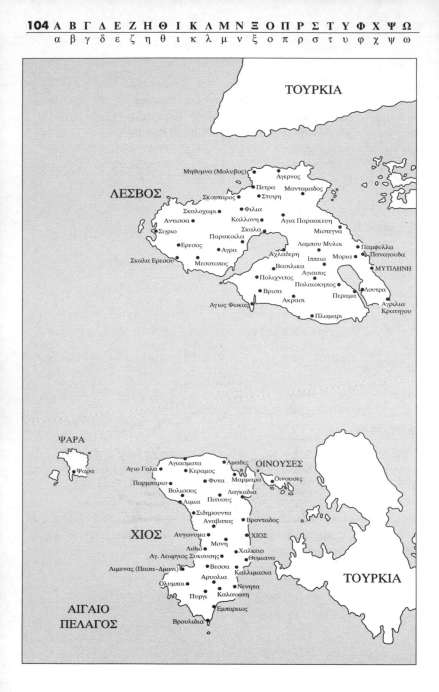

Anagrams

Mike and Lisa are getting ready to leave for Athens airport where a flight is waiting to get them home. They find that, in order to get there, they have to reverse their outward journey. They first need a boat, then a taxi and finally, an aeroplane. Their transportation is written below in capitals. Unfortunately, however, some of the letters have been scrambled (did we mention that anagram is a Greek word? – ανάγραμμο). To help you unscramble them, we have provided a key, BUT the key, which is in lower case letters, has been partially destroyed, so that some letters are missing. See if you can match the missing letters with the scrambled words so that you can write out the word in full:

ΚΑΒΑΡΙ   _ αρα _ _

ΑΕΠΑΡΛΟΝΟ   αερ _ _ λα _ _

ΙΞΤΑ   _ _ ξ _

Solutions

They all sound the same!

1 χαρτί = paper
2 ΧΑΡΤΗΣ = map
3 βάζο = vase
4 ΒΑΖΩ = I put
5 κριτής = judge
6 ΚΡΗΤΗ = Crete
7 κρίνω = I judge
8 ΚΡΙΝΟΣ = lily
9 φύλο = sex (M or F)
10 ΦΙΛΟΣ = friend (M)

Exercise 1

1 ΧΑΡΤΙ = paper
2 χάρτης = map
3 ΒΑΖΟ = vase
4 βάζω = I put
5 ΚΡΙΤΗΣ = judge
6 κρήτη = Crete
7 ΚΡΙΝΩ = I judge
8 κρίνος = lily
9 ΦΥΛΟ = sex (M or F)
10 φίλος = friend (M)

Exercise 2

Souvenirs

1 Things you drink	2 Things you eat	3 Mementoes
ούζο	σοκολάτα	φωτογραφία
Ελληνικός καφές	Ελληνικό λάδι	μπλουζάκι
ρετσίνα	γλυκά	άγαλμα

1 Things you drink	2 Things you eat	3 Mementoes
πορτοκαλάδα		σημαία
μπύρα		χάρτης
		βιβλία
		εισητήρια
		ψώνια
		δραχμές
		κασέτα
		τσάντα
		εφημερίδα

Greek weather

Sunny	αίθριος
Occasional cloud	άστατος
Heavy cloud	συννεφιά
Rain	βροχή
Thunderstorm	καταιγίδα
Snow	χιόνι
Fog	ομίχλη

From the same weather report write in capitals the names of the large cities, outside Greece, which have a temperature higher than London:

ΠΑΡΙΣΙ

ΡΩΜΗ

ΖΥΡΙΧΗ

ΜΟΣΧΑ

Now write in capitals the names of the Greek towns which have the same temperature as Rome:

ΝΑΜΙΑ

ΠΑΤΡΑ

Now write the name of the town whose temperature is nearest that of London:

ΜΟΣΧΑ

Acronyms

Ιησούς Χριστός, Θεού Υιός, Σωτήρ

Postcards

ΤΟ ΔΙΑΜΕΡΙΣΜΑ ΗΤΑΝ ΠΟΛΥ ΩΡΑΙΟ.

ΕΥΧΑΡΙΣΤΩ ΓΙΑ ΟΛΑ.

ΛΙΣΑ

The map

ΛΕΣΒΟΣ	ΜΥΤΙΛΗΝΗ
ΧΙΟΣ	ΧΙΟΣ
ΨΑΡΑ	ΨΑΡΑ

Anagrams

καράβι

αεροπλάνο

ταξί

ΓΛΩΣΣΑΡΙΟ
GLOSSARY

In the next few pages we will give you all the words you've encountered in units 6–10, along with their definition and some cultural background. Although this book is about the alphabet, it is natural, as you become more proficient, to want to try your new language skills out as much as you can. To help you, we have also provided a handy dictionary, or λεξικόν, at the end of the book. This gives you all the words you've encountered in both their capital and small case forms, along with the definitions and the letters of the alphabet, and a few extra, associated words which you may find useful.

Unit 6

Μεγάλα – γ   plural, big, large. The Greek word for big has lent itself in English to such words as megalomaniac and the now popularly accepted slang prefix 'mega' (as in '*Beginner's Greek Script* is a megabook and the glossary at the end of Unit 10 is mega!')

Μικρά – κ   plural, small, little. As with 'big', the Greek word for small has found many applications in English, where we have imported derivatives such as microcosm, microscopic, micron (a unit of measurement in the sub-atomic realm) and microscope.

Ντεντέκτιβ – ντ   detective, though the word in Greek is popularly applied to private investigators and sleuths more than to police detectives. Peculiarly perhaps, the 'detective novel', in Greek, is called the 'police novel' or more popularly, 'police story'.

Πιτσαρία – τσ   a pizza restaurant. Italy started out as an Ancient Greek colony (as did France, incidentally) but in the course of time has come to influence a lot of the cultural aspects of modern Grece. This is reflected in the popularity of pizza and spaghetti in the Greek menu.

Ουζερί – ου   a place where you would go to drink ouzo and have a meze. Modern ουζερί, in Athens and the islands, these days also offer live entertainment and a more varied drinks menu, though food, traditionally, remains fairly rudimentary in its variety in so far as you still cannot get a full meal there.

Μπυραρία – μπ   a place where you would go to drink mainly beer. These places were tremendously popular during the 60s and 70s when beer was the drink of choice of the 'flower power generation' in Greece. They are now slowly disappearing.

Καφετερία – φ   a Greek café

Οπωροπολείο – ω   a fruit shop. It's a compound word from Οπωρικά (green produce) and πουλάω (I sell). Greek fruit shops portray an element of Greek life which sadly is, slowly disappearing. They display a lot of their produce in the wooden crates it comes in, outside the shop. When the shop was closed, the owners would cover the produce with tarpaulin but still leave it outside, overnight and unattended! There would be nothing missing when they opened the next day. This is a practice which is slowly dying out as specialised fruit shops become fewer in number and some of the less savoury aspects of modern life catch up in Greece.

Χρυσοχοείο – ει   jeweller's. It literally means 'gold-maker'. The Greek for gold is Χρυσός. Greek jewellery has a tradition which goes back more than 3,000 years. Greek gold jewellery is slightly heavier and darker in colour than gold jewellery in other parts of the world because Greek jewellers work with either 18 or 22 karat gold, not with 9kt.

Ξενοδοχείο – ει   hotel. A compound word (Ξενος = foreigner and δοχειο = container) literally meaning 'a container for foreigners'! It has loaned itself to words such as xenophobia (a fear of strangers).

Αρτοπωλείο – ω   bakery. Traditionally, in Greece, every neighbourhood had its own bakery where bread was freshly stone-baked on a daily basis.

Ζαχαροπλαστείο – ει   patisserie. Greek sweets make use of a lot of cream which itself is sweetened. As a result they seem to have been made with UHT cream, though this is not the case.

Εστιατόρειο – ει   restaurant

Κινηματογράφος – η   cinema. Literally translated, it means 'Writing in motion'.

Ντισκοτέκ – ντ   disco. While this is obviously the Greek equivalent of an imported word from English, there is a school of thought which says that the Greeks originally exported it to England in its Greek original which is δισκοθήκη = Discotheque. This is a compound word meaning 'container for music records'!

Φαρμακείο – ει   pharmacy/chemist. Originally it took its name from the word φάρμακι meaning poison, as in ancient Greece, many of the cures effected were through the use of diluted concoctions of otherwise poisonous substances.

Ταχυδρομείο – ει   post office. Given the problems that the Greek postal service has had over the past ten years in delivering things on time, the literal translation of this word (i.e. fast road) may be slightly ironic!

Φαγητό – η   food

Ψωμί – ψ   bread

Χρυσός – ς   gold. Chrysanthemum (gold flower), and chrysalis (golden) which originally referred to a gold coloured butterfly pupa, are English derivatives.

Γλυκά – γ   sweets (plural)

Δωμάτιο – δ   room

Φίλμ – μ   movie/film. English film titles do not always translate well into Greek, so many films appear with titles which bear no resemblance to the original.

Καφέ – κ   coffee

Ασπιρίνη – π   aspirin

Χορός – ρ   dance. This is directly linked to the English words chorus and choir. In ancient Greek plays the chorus and choir both sang and danced in the background in order to fill the transitional gaps in the play, or to tell the historical background, against which the drama of the play was unfolding.

Γραμματόσημα – μ   stamps. It literally means 'a sign for a letter'.

Απογευματηνή – ν   Initially, a daily newspaper appearing only in Athens (as most papers did at the time), it's now a national paper.

Ακρόπολη – λ   another influential Athenian daily paper. Others like it are Μεσημεριανή (lit. noon paper), Σημεριανή (Today's paper), Κύρηκος (translated as the perhaps slightly ambitious 'Gospel') and Εθνική (National).

Πελοπόννησος – ν   a regional newspaper. As the name suggests it is limited to the Peloponnese area.

Γλυκός – ν   adjective meaning 'sweet', as in a sweet coffee, etc.

Σιδηρόδρομος – δ   railway. Railways did not come until fairly late in Greece and they are not the fastest means of travel across the country, though they are certainly amongst the cheapest. The word itself is a compound word and it means iron road.

Σίδηρος – ρ   iron

Δρόμος – μ   road. While this word is used to describe a road, it is not the word you will see on the names of Greek road signs. This is due to tradition. We give you the word, for reference, in the dictionary at the end of this book.

Τραίνο – αι   train

Λεοφορείο – ει   bus. Greece has an excellent public transport network. Although bus stops themselves are not always well signposted, the buses do run every fifteen minutes and the cost is low.

Αυτοκίνητο – αυ   car, literally 'automatic motion'. There is no indigenous car industry in Greece and all makes have to be imported. Because Greece has a high level of tax avoidance, the Greek Inland Revenue uses car ownership to gauge levels of income (and therefore tax liability). The formula used in this instance centres on the size of the engine of the car you buy. This is only one reason why smaller cars are so popular in Greece.

Φεριμπότ – μπ   ferry (boat). A word imported into Greek.

Ελικόπτερο – λ   helicopter. While purists will argue that this is clearly a word brought into Greek from English, it has been pointed out that the word for the rotor blades (Ελικας) of the helicopter is Greek, and did come first.

Φορτηγό – Φ   truck

Πούλμαν – ου   coach

Τελεφερίκ – λ   cable car

Υποβρύχιο – β   submarine

Τάνξ – ξ   tank

Αεροπλάνο – ρ   aeroplane

Ταξί – ξ   taxi

Τυροπωλείο – υ   a place that sells only cheese or dairy products.

Γαλακτοπωλείο – ει   a place which sells exclusively milk products.

Βιβλιοπωλείο – β   a bookshop. Though the ancient Greeks were in love with literature, there never was a thriving book trade at the time. The main reason for this is one of cost. In the days of ancient Greece, most writing was done on wax tablets, where letters were literally scratched on dark-coloured wax which then allowed a lighter coloured wood background to show through. Tablets were bound together using metal rings, looped through holes in their edges. The first organised, systematic buying and selling of books developed in Alexandria in the 2nd Century BC primarily because of the influence of its famous library, run by Ptolemy.

Γάλα – γ   milk. Funnily enough, the Greek word for milk is responsible for the naming of the Galaxy (Milky Way), where the first observers thought the broad band of stars through its middle looked like a streak of spilled milk!

Πορτοκάλι – π   orange. The same word is used for both the fruit and the colour, though the stress in the latter is shifted to the very last letter.

Ντομάτες – ντ   tomatoes

Μήλα – μ   apples

Τυρί – τ   cheese. The main types of cheese you buy in Greece are the produce of either sheep or goat's milk. Until the early 1900s there were three types of cheese which were described according to their hardness as soft, medium, and hard. The 'hard' cheese would be cured in the open air for quite a long time. It was salty and good only for use in σαγανάκι where it would be accompanied by ouzo, or grated and sprinkled on food.

Μπουκάλι – μπ   bottle. Bottled wine in a taverna is a fairly novel concept in Greece, though restaurants have had them a lot longer. Traditionally, tavernas serve their wine straight from the barrel.

Κρασί – κ   wine

Βιβλίο – Β   book. The word has lent itself to such usage as bibliography (writing about books or a list of books) and the Bible.

Φέτα – φ   a soft, white Greek cheese, made out of goat's milk, with a distinctive flavour and texture. Different regions of Greece produce different types of feta cheese.

Ουίσκυ – ου   whisky

Καρπούζι – ζ   water melon. Water melons in Greece are abundant during the summer months, where in many places they are sold from the back of farm trucks by the side of roads or near beaches.

Γιαούρτι – γ   yoghurt. Greek yoghurt is a very rich, full-fat yoghurt and is the usual dessert to a Greek meal. It is served sprinkled lightly with cinnamon, or topped with honey. Greek yoghurt is made from the milk of goats or sheep, not cows. Greece doesn't have many cows as its mountainous terrain cannot sustain the grasslands necessary for dairy herds.

Σοκολάτα – Σ   chocolate

Βούτηρο – η   butter

Πακέτο – π   packet

Μπισκότα – μπ   biscuits

Λεμόνια – λ   lemons

Μπύρα – μπ   beer

Unit 7

Τρώμε – ω   We eat/We are eating. Because eating out is so cheap, Greece has a thriving night-life. People think nothing of going out for a meal at least twice a week. Although tourist restaurants open early, Greek restaurant hours are somewhat later than ours, as many Greeks would not consider having their evening meal before ten o'clock!

Εξω – ξ   out. The word exodus is derived directly from this.

Μενού – ου   menu. A word clearly imported into Greek from English.

Γεμιστά – Γ stuffed tomatoes (usually). They are cooking tomatoes with the insides emptied and the skin stuffed with rice and (depending in which region you have them) mince.

Πατάτες – Π potatoes and also, chips. Potatoes were introduced in Greece in the late 1800s by Ioannis Metaxas. They were initially called γεώμηλα (earth-apples) because of their appearance and the then hungry populace, suspicious of anything introduced by the government, refused to eat them. The story goes that the Greek governor ordered mountains of potatoes to be piled high in public squares under guard. The guards were given specific instructions to look the other way should anyone try to steal them. Some of them were indeed stolen and presumably cooked and eaten. Word of mouth soon spread and the rest is history.

Φούρνου – φ oven baked. Quite a lot of food is cooked that way in Greece.

Τηγανητές – η fried (usually refers to chips)

Παστίτσιο – τσ a pasta and mincemeat dish, the origins of which lie more in the East than Greece.

Μακαρονάδα – δ cooked spaghetti

Μπριζόλα – μπ steak. The traditional Greek diet is low on meat and very rich in vegetable dishes. Historically this is due to what was seasonally available to a population with no access to refrigeration.

Χοιρινή – χ pork

Μοσχαρήσια – ρ beef

Κεφτέδες – Κ meatballs. Greek mince is made directly from prime cuts of meat which are then minced, so there is no compromise in quality.

Σαλάτα – τ salad

Χωριάτικη – Χ This is what is usually known as Greek salad, though the more literal translation is 'village salad'. Traditional Greek salad is rich in olive oil (a handy source of carbohydrates) and it also contains feta cheese, tomatoes, cucumbers and olives. It is, in many respects, a meal in itself and the olive oil that's in it is usually soaked up by bread and then eaten.

Μαρούλι – μ lettuce

Φάστ Φούντ – Φ   fast food. Quite a few English words have been adopted by Greek as the globalisation of a 'fast' lifestyle makes itself felt.

Χάμπουρκερ – X   hamburger

Σάντουιτς – Σ   The concept of the sandwich is relatively new in Greek culture and still considered something of a novelty in certain remote parts.

Σαλάτα – σ   salad. Interestingly, because the Greek salad has a lot of ingredients which need to be tossed, the phrase 'You've made a salad of it' is identical in meaning to the English 'you've made a hash of it'.

Σως – ω   sauce. It usually refers to tomato sauce.

Κετσάπ – τσ   ketchup

Μουστάρδα – δ   mustard. Greek mustard is very much like French in that it is not very hot. It is usually served with chips.

Μπέικον – μπ   bacon

Κοτόπουλο – τ   chicken

Καρότο – ρ   carrot

Παγωτό – ω   ice cream. Home-made Greek ice-cream makes use of full-fat milk and cream and is very rich.

Unit 8

Στο – Σ   at, in or on depending on, usage and context.

Μουσείο – ει   museum. Greek museums, despite the wealth of antiquities they have in storage, have been chronically underfunded. It is only in recent years that the government has begun to redress the balance. A lot of preservation work is being undertaken and more items are being put on display.

Δευτέρα – ευ   Monday. Literally translated, it means second day of the week.

Τρίτη – ρ   Tuesday, third day of the week.

Τετάρτη – η   Wednesday, fourth day of the week.

Πέμπτη – π   Thursday, fifth day of the week.

Παρασκευή – ευ   Friday. This means 'day of preparation'.

Σάββατο – β   Saturday, a word which bears more than a passing resemblance to the Sabbath.

Κυριακή – η   Sunday. Literally translated, it means the Lord's day.

Ακρη – ρ   edge

Πόλη – η   town or city. The word metropolitan would not mean what it does today without the Greek word for city.

Ποδήλατο – δ   bicycle

Βέσπα – Β   a small motorcycle (taken from the Italian Vespa). Because they are cheap to obtain and run, and practical to use in the narrow streets of many Greek seaside towns and villages, small motorcycles like these have become a major source of noise pollution in recent years.

Τζίπ – τζ   jeep

Καράβι – ρ   ship

Τζατζίκι – τζ   a Greek garlic and yoghurt dip. Like many similar dishes, it originally came from the East and became part of Greek cuisine when Greece was a tiny part of the Ottoman Empire.

Αυγά – αυ   eggs. Battery farming is not yet in operation in Greece. Most eggs are produced, sold and bought locally, usually in open-air markets.

Ζάχαρη – Z   sugar. Saccharine is a sugar substitute and was so named when discovered because of its sweet taste!

Βανίλλια – Β   vanilla

Αμερικάνικο – Α   American (adjective)

Δολλάριο – Δ   dollar

Ρώσικο Ρούβλι – Ρ   the Russian Rouble. Greece and Russia were once very closely connected through the Orthodox Church and there used to be links between the Russian Royal family and the Greek one.

Ιταλική Λίρα – Ι   the Italian Lira

Ισπανική Πετσέτα – τσ   the Spanish Peseta

Ελληνική Δραχμή – λ   the Greek Drachma

Αθήνα – θ   Athens. The capital of Greece. Legend says that when Athens was built it was such a bright, vibrant city that the Olympian gods queued to become its patron. Of them all, Athena (The Goddess of Wisdom), and Poseidon (The God of the Ocean) won, and they each had to compete for the privilege. The contest was to give the city a gift to be judged by its elders. Poseidon was first and he struck the ground with his trident and made an eternal spring flow. Athena gave the city the olive tree. Of the two, hers was deemed to be the more valuable gift and the city was named after her, though Poseidon's spring still flows, and if you drink Athens water, you will always want to return to the city.

Μαδρίτη – η   Madrid

Παρίσι – Π   Paris

Ουάσινγκτον – ου   the city of Washington DC

Μεξικό – ξ   the city of Mexico

Λονδίνο – Λ   London

Unit 9

Ταξιδάκια – δ   small trips or excursions. Quite a few Greek words use a special ending to make the word a 'diminutive', which slightly alters its meaning.

Δωδεκάνησα – Δ   Dodecanese is the English form. Literally translated, it means 'twelve islands', because there were twelve islands in that group.

Δελφοί – οι   Delphi. The famous temple of the oracle which was called the 'navel of the world' as it was thought to lie at the centre of the known world.

Σάμος – μ   Samos, one of the Aegean Sea islands. It was one of the most important islands of the ancient world. Two of its most famous residents were Aesop, author of Aesop's Fables, and the mathematician Pythagoras.

Λαός – Λ   people or crowd

Λάδι – δ   oil, frequently olive oil. Most Greek cooking is done in olive oil.

Ωμέγα – Ω   omega. The final letter of the Greek alphabet.

Γκρίζο – Γκ   grey

Αγγούρι – γγ   cucumber. This is often used in Greek salads.

Άγγελος – γγ   angel. Directly from the Greek, we have borrowed the word angel, as well as archangel.

Αγγίζω – ω   I touch, I'm touching

Αγγλος – γγ   Englishman

Ελευθεροτυπία – ευ   one more of the Athenian newspapers. It is now released as a national paper. A literal translation of the name means 'free press'.

Οικονομία – οι   economy

Πολιτική – η   politics. Greek politics is a very passionate, often polarising, affair with the two main parties at the moment being left and right of centre.

Σπορ – Σ   sport. A word imported from English.

Πουλόβερ – ου   pullover

Δέκα – Δ   ten

Ιανουαρίου – ου   January's

Ευρώ – ευ   euro

Ρεκόρ – ρ   record

Κρήτη – η   Crete, the largest of the Greek islands and one with a history of rebellion. To date it is the only place in Greece where, despite the strict gun-control laws of the country, people openly carry guns and knives strapped to their belts.

Ελλάδα – λ   Greece

Αμόκ – κ   amok. Another word which has been imported directly from the English.

Αγορές – γ   markets

Unit 10

Σουβενίρ – Σ   souvenir

Ομοιο – οι   the same, identical

Φωνή – η   voice. This is the reason the first record players were called phonographs (writing in voice), and tele(afar)phone(voice) also took its name from this word.

Ομόφωνη – η   homophonc

Χαρτί – χ   paper

Χάρτης – Χ   map

Βάζο – ζ   vase

Βάζω – Ω   I put, I'm putting

Κρίτης – γ   judge

Κρίνω – ω   I judge, I'm judging

Κρίνος – ν   lily

Φύλο – Φ   sex (M and F)

Φίλος – λ   friend

Χείρα – ει   formal Greek for hand

Χοίρα – οι   sow, female pig

Χήρα – η   widow

Αγαλμα – γ   statue. Ancient Greeks actually believed that the more detailed a statue was, the closer to being alive it became. As a result they worked very hard on their statues to create detail which the world was not to see again until the opening years of the Renaissance.

Φωτογραφία – Φ   photograph. Literally meaning, 'writing in light'.

Μπλουζάκι – μπ   T-shirt

Σημαία – αι   flag. The Greek flag with its distinctive white and blue stripes and Greek cross is a code of the national anthem in Greece. The number of stripes on the flag is equal to the number of verses in the national anthem.

Εφημερίδα – Ε   newspaper. Originally, newspapers in Greece were either government controlled or closely affiliated with a particular political party, which then financed them. This situation has now changed.

Εισητήρια – ει   tickets. It used to be that you could buy tickets on Greek buses from a conductor. In the mid-80s this changed, and you had to buy your ticket from a designated place, long before you boarded a bus. This created an interesting situation when it became apparent that the number of designated places selling bus tickets were few and far between. This situation has now, largely, been rectified and you can buy bus tickets from any street-corner kiosk.

Κασέτα – κ   cassette

Τσάντα – τσ   handbag

Θερμοκρασία – Θ   temperature

Θερμόμετρο – μ   thermometer, literally, nothing more than a 'counter' of temperature

Ονομα – ο   name. Greek names are usually taken from the Greek Orthodox calendar, which is the reason why, on certain islands which have a patron saint, a lot of people seem to have the same first name.

Ακρόνυμο – υ   acronym

Ιχθύς – θ   fish, but also the acronym by which Christians became known to each other, and Christianity became recognised.

Ιυσούς – ου   Jesus

Χριστός – τ   Christ

Θεού – ου   God's

Υιός – ι   formal Greek for son

Σωτήρας – ω   saviour

Καλαματιανό – α   Greek dance from the area of Kalamata, a region also renowned for the quality of its olives and the richness of its olive oil.

Συρτάκι – κ   modern Greek dance. It became really popular during the early 1960s when a less athletic but equally communal dance to Καλαματιανό was being sought.

Κρητικός – η   As the name implies this is a Cretan dance, and like most Cretan dances is, essentially, a war dance. When performed by trained dancers, the lead dancer has a knife in one hand which he wields about him as he jumps and gyrates through the air, held and aided by his second, who holds onto him by one end of a handkerchief.

Κλέφτικο – φ   a Greek dance dating back to the times when Greek rebels fought the Ottoman army.

Ρεμπέτικο – μπ   Unusually for a Greek dance, this is a solitary dance. Its roots are to be found in the Athens of the 1920s and 30s where the movement of the Ρεμπέτη got under way. Those who subscribed to it saw themselves as loners in a strange world, constantly fighting against the establishment through conscious non-conformity.

Δημοτικό – μ   a popular Greek dance which has many variations in different regions all over Greece. It is characterised by its upbeat, quick-step music and lively steps.

Ζελατίνα – Z   jelly

Καρτ-ποστάλ – ρ   postcard. This is an imported word from the French.

Ανάγραμμο – μ   anagram

Αίθριος – θ   clement, usually referring to weather

Αστατος – σ   unsettled

Συννεφιά – σ   heavy cloud. Greece has 256 sun-drenched days a year!

Βροχή – B   rain. Most of the rainfall in Greece takes place during winter.

Καταιγίδα – κ   storm

Χιόνι – χ   snow. Even Greece experiences snowfall in winter, with some mountain villages being cut off for weeks on end. The botanical name for the early flowering small blue, pink or white bulb 'glory of the snow' is chionodoxa, from χιόνι + δόξα (glory).

Ομίχλη – χ   fog

11 ΧΡΗΣΙΜΕΣ ΛΕΞΕΙΣ
USEFUL WORDS

We're almost there now. Your survival guide to the Greek alphabet, Greek culture and Greek way of life is almost complete. Below are some bits and pieces which you will find useful for reference. Dip in and out as necessary and don't be afraid to ask if you're not sure about the meaning of anything when in Greece.

It's a good sign – finding your way around

In most countries, anywhere you go you are bombarded by signs, and Greece is no exception. So that you will feel at home, and also perhaps avoid some potentially embarrassing situations, we have provided a list of some of the most common signs which you may meet or need.

ΓΥΝΑΙΚΩΝ	LADIES
ΑΝΔΡΩΝ	GENTLEMEN
ΚΙΝΔΥΝΟΣ	DANGER
ΣΤΑΣΙΣ	STOP
ΑΠΑΓΟΡΕΥΕΤΑΙ	PROHIBITED, IT IS FORBIDDEN
ΕΠΙΤΡΕΠΕΤΑΙ	PERMITTED, IT IS ALLOWED
ΑΝΟΙΚΤΟ	OPEN
ΚΛΕΙΣΤΟ	CLOSED
ΣΥΡΑΤΕ	PULL
ΩΘΗΣΑΤΕ	PUSH
ΕΙΣΟΔΟΣ	ENTRANCE
ΕΞΟΔΟΣ	EXIT

ΔΙΑΒΑΤΗΡΙΑ	PASSPORTS
ΤΟΥΑΛΕΤΑ	TOILET

Taking the lift

ΥΠΟΓ/ΥΠΟΓΕΙΟΝ	BASEMENT
ΙΣ/ΙΣΟΓΕΙΟΝ	GROUND FLOOR
ΗΜ/ΗΜΙΟΡΟΦΟΣ	MEZZANINE FLOOR
1ος	1st floor
2ος	2nd floor
3ος	3rd floor
4ος	4th floor

Forging good relationships

It isn't absolutely essential for you to remember these last two signs, but it would be very good for your εγω, and give a boost to the cause of international friendship, to be able to recognise that

ΚΑΛΩΣΟΡΙΣΑΤΕ ΣΤΗΝ ΕΛΛΑΔΑ means *Welcome to Greece* and
ΚΑΛΩΣΟΡΙΣΑΤΕ ΣΤΗΝ ΚΥΠΡΟ means *Welcome to Cyprus*.

It all adds up – Greek numbers

0	μηδέν	15	δεκαπέντε
1	ένα	16	δεκαέξι
2	δύο	17	δεκαεφτά
3	τρείς	18	δεκαοχτώ
4	τέσσερεις	19	δεκαεννιά
5	πέντε	20	είκοσι
6	έξι	21	εικοσι ένα
7	εφτά or επτα	22	εικοσι δύο
8	οχτώ or οκτω	23	εικοσι τρία
9	εννιά or εννεα	24	εικοσι τέσσερα
10	δέκα	25	εικοσι πέντε
11	έντεκα	26	εικοσι έξι
12	δώδεκα	27	εικοσι εφτά
13	δεκατρία	28	εικοσι οχτώ
14	δεκατέσσερα	29	εικοσι εννιά

You have already met the two ways of writing the Greek for seven, eight and nine, and you can use either version whenever these digits crop up. Twenty-seven, for example can be either εικοσι εφτα or εικοσι επτα.

There are several other numbers that for grammatical reasons have more than one form in Greek, but we aren't proposing to confuse you by giving them here. If, as we hope, our introduction to Greek script has shown you that the alphabet is nowhere near as hard as it's cracked up to be, we are fairly confident that you'll take our word for it when we say that if you go on to learn more Greek, you'll soon know which form to use, and anyway, everyone will understand you even if you do use the wrong one by mistake.

30	τριαντα	70	εβδομήντα
40	σαράντα	80	ογδόντα
50	πενήντα	90	ενενήτα
60	εξήντα		

To make the numbers from thirty-one to ninety-nine, follow the same pattern as shown for twenty-one to twenty-nine, substituting the appropriate digits.

100 εκατό (Note that in English we say '*One* hundred' but in Greek you leave out the 'one'.)

Just when you thought that you were getting the hang of this, some ancient Greek mathematician had to come along and complicate things! If you want to use two hundred, three hundred or any of the hundreds up to and including nine hundred, the word for hundred changes to -κοσια. The preceding word also changes slightly, but is still recognisable. If you forget, for example, that it's εξακοσια and not εξι-κοσια when you collect the key at the hotel, you will (probably!) still end up in the right room.

200	διακόσια
300	τριακόσια
400	τετρακόσια
500	πεντακόσια
600	εξακόσια
700	εφτακόσια
800	οχτακόσια
900	εννιακόσια

Thousands are much easier to manage. Mike and Lisa introduced you to χιλια (thousand) and χιλιαδες (thousands) so all you do is combine words that you already know how to make.

1000	χίλια (once again, it's just 'thousand' not '*one* thousand')
2000	δύο χιλιάδες
3000	τρείς χιλιάδες
4000	τέσσερεις χιλιάδες
5000	πέντε χιλιάδες
6000	έξι χιλιάδες
7000	εφτά χιλιάδες
8000	οχτώ χιλιάδες
9000	εννιά χιλιάδες

1 000 000   ένα εκατομμύριο

We could go on forever of course, but you probably have enough numbers here to keep you going for a while!

Keeping track of time the Greek way

Greeks have a peculiar notion of time. Morning (πρωι) in Greece starts pretty much about the same time as it does everywhere else in the world, but noon (μεσημερι) does not really start until about 1 p.m. and it goes on until 4 p.m. As soon as you get past the 4 p.m. watershed, afternoon takes over and this lasts until sundown (which varies slightly depending on the time of year) and then you have night (βραδι or νυχτα). While Greeks are perfectly well aware of this arrangement, many visitors to the country are not. Greeks don't know this. Arrange to meet in a local in the 'afternoon' wihout naming a precise time and you could be in for a lengthy wait.

Days of the week

Κυριακή	Sunday
Δευτέρα	Monday
Τρίτη	Tuesday
Τετάρη	Wednesday
Πέμπτη	Thursday
Παρασκεύη	Friday
Σαββάτο	Saturday

Months of the year

Ιανουάριος	January
Φεβρουάριος	February
Μάρτιος	March
Απρίλιος	April
Μάιος	May
Ιούνιος	June
Ιούλιος	July
Αύγουστος	August
Σεπτέμβριος	September
Οκτώβριος	October
Νοέμβριος	November
Δεκέμβριος	December

Seasons

άνοιξη	spring
καλοκαίρι	summer
φθινόπωρο	autumn
χειμώνας	winter

The four corners of the earth

Βορράς	north
Νότος	south
Ανατολή	east
Δύση	west

Relationships

Greeks believe in extended families and many live very close to their relatives. Some of the terms used to describe family relationships are probably familiar, some, however, will be strange enough to require a little attention.

πατέρας	father
μητέρα	mother
γονιός	parent
γονείς	parents

αδελφός	brother
αδελφή	sister
εξάδελφος	cousin (male)
εξαδέλφη	cousin (female)
παππούς	grandfather
γιαγιά	grandmother
εγγονός	grandson
εγγονή	granddaughter

A BRIEF HISTORY OF ANCIENT GREECE

'The glory that was Greece', in the words of Edgar Allan Poe, was short-lived and confined to a very small geographic area. Yet, thanks to the development of the Byzantine Empire, which succeeded it, and its absorption by the Roman Empire, which conquered it, it has influenced the growth of Western civilization far out of proportion to its size and duration.

The Greece that Poe praised was primarily Athens during its Golden Age in the 5th century BC. Strictly speaking, the state was Attica; Athens was its heart. The English poet John Milton called Athens 'the eye of Greece, mother of arts and eloquence'. Athens was the city-state in which the arts,

philosophy and democracy flourished. At least it was the city that attracted those who wanted to work, speak, and think in an environment of freedom. In the rarefied atmosphere of Athens were born ideas about human nature and political society that are fundamental to the Western world today.

Athens may have been the brightest of its city-states but it was not the whole of Greece. Sparta, Corinth, Thebes and Thessalonica were but a few of the many other city-states that existed on the rocky and mountainous peninsula at the southern end of the Balkans. Each city-state was an independent political unit, and each vied with the others for power and wealth. These city-states planted Greek colonies in Asia Minor, on many islands in the Aegean Sea, and in southern Italy and Sicily.

The story of ancient Greece began between 1900 and 1600 BC. At that time the Greeks – or Hellenes, as they called themselves – were simple nomadic herdsmen. Their language shows that they were a branch of the Indo-European-speaking peoples. They came from the grasslands east of the Caspian Sea, driving their flocks and herds before them. They entered the peninsula from the north, one small group after another.

The first invaders were the blue-eyed, fair-haired Achaeans of whom Homer wrote. The dark-haired, stockier but war-like Dorians came perhaps three or four centuries later and subjugated the Achaean tribes. Other tribes, the Aeolians and the Ionians, found homes chiefly on the islands in the Aegean Sea and on the coast of Asia Minor.

The land that these tribes invaded – the Aegean Basin – was the site of a well-developed Aegean civilization. The people who lived there had cities and palaces. They used gold and bronze and made pottery and paintings.

The Greek invaders were still in the barbarian stage. They plundered and destroyed the Aegean cities. Gradually, as they settled and intermarried with the people they conquered, they absorbed some of the Aegean culture.

Little is known of the earliest stages of Greek settlement. The invaders probably moved southward from their pasturelands along the Danube, bringing their families and primitive goods in rough oxcarts. Along the way they grazed their herds. In the spring they stopped long enough to plant and harvest a single crop. Gradually they settled down to form communities ruled by kings and elders.

The background of the two great Greek epics – the 'Iliad' and the 'Odyssey' – is the background of the Age of Kings. These epics depict the simple, warlike life of the early Greeks. The Achaeans had excellent weapons and sang stirring songs. Such luxuries as they possessed, however – gorgeous robes, jewellery, elaborate metalwork – they bought from the Phoenician traders.

The 'Iliad' tells how Greeks from many city-states – among them, Sparta, Athens, Thebes, and Argos – joined forces to fight their common foe, Troy in Asia Minor. In historical times the Greek city-states were again able to combine when the power of Persia threatened them. However, this diversity, which produced the cultural wealth of ancient Greece, was also its curse, for it never became a nation. The only patriotism the ancient Greek knew was loyalty to his city. The size of each city-state, at the time,

did not make for much more than 10,000 people. Athens was probably the only Greek city-state with more than 20,000 citizens and it ruled mostly by its size and glitter; its gravity in the affairs of the city-states around it was counterbalanced by the military might of Sparta.

Only in a few cases did a city-state push its holdings beyond very narrow limits. Athens held the whole plain of Attica, and most of the Attic villagers were Athenian citizens. Argos conquered the plain of Argolis. Sparta made a conquest of Laconia and part of the fertile plain of Messenia. The conquered people were subjects, not citizens. Thebes attempted to be the ruling city of Boeotia but never quite succeeded.

Similar city-states were found all over the Greek world, which had flung its outposts throughout the Aegean Basin and even beyond. There were Greeks in all the islands of the Aegean. Among these islands was Thasos, famous for its gold mines. Samothrace, Imbros, and Lemnos were long occupied by Athenian colonists. Other Aegean islands colonized by Greeks included Lesbos, the home of the poet Sappho; Scyros, the island of Achilles; and Chios, Samos and Rhodes. Also settled by Greeks were the nearer-lying Cyclades – so called (from the Greek word for 'circle') because they encircled the sacred island of Delos – and the southern island of Crete.

The western shores of Asia Minor were fringed with Greek colonies, reaching out past the Propontis (Sea of Marmara) and the Bosporus to the northern and southern shores of the Euxine, or Black Sea. In Africa there were, among others, the colony of Cyrene, now the site of a town in Libya, and the trading post of Naucratis in Egypt. Sicily too was colonized by the Greeks, and there and in southern Italy so many colonies were planted that this region came to be known as Magna Graecia (Great Greece). Pressing farther still, the Greeks founded the city of Massilia, now Marseilles, France.

Separated by barriers of sea and mountain, by local pride and jealousy, the various independent city-states never conceived the idea of uniting the Greek-speaking world into a single political unit. They formed alliances only when some powerful city-state embarked on a career of conquest and attempted to make itself leader of the rest. Many influences made for unity – a common language, a common religion, a common literature, similar customs, the religious leagues and festivals, the Olympic Games – but even in time of foreign invasion it was difficult to induce the cities to act together, a fact which they were to regret in later times, when other, more powerful, invaders cast their eyes towards the glitter that was Greece, and decided that the time had come to make her theirs.

If the Greek language is as complex and as beautiful as it is today, it owes a lot to this tumultuous history. It is to the discipline-loving Spartans for example that we owe the sense of the austere (hence the word Spartan). Similarly the Delphic Oracle of Pythia with her cryptic replies gave us the word 'pithy' for a short, to-the-point phrase.

Similarly, the Greek alphabet you have been studying bears traces of the history it has passed through. The difference in sounds, the funny-looking letters and the letter combinations to make different sounds, all betray the Egyptian and Phoenician influence of the past. They show traces of Byzantinian dabbling and reveal, at times, the subtlety that made Byzantinian politics the deadly power game it was.

To study the alphabet of any language is to launch oneself upon a tide of history and feel the beauty of the past. It is also but the first step in a journey which is just beginning.

12 ΕΠΙΛΟΓΟΣ
EPILOGUE

We entered this book with the prologue, (from the thoroughly Greek word πρόλογος, προ = before + λόγος = word), so we now have to make our exit with the equally Greek επίλογος (επι = on top of/in addition). By now, reading or writing the Greek alphabet will be a piece of cake, and you may want to start finding out more for yourself, instead of relying on us to choose what you are going to learn. This means that, even if you haven't already done so, you'll soon need to use a dictionary. As you've probably noticed, Greek alphabetical order is slightly different from that of English, and this can make using a dictionary frustrating until you get used to its idiosyncrasies, or ιδιοσυγκρασίες, as the Greek would say. It is, for example, somewhat disconcerting for the English speaker to find Z popping up next to E in a Greek dictionary.

To help you, we've provided some exercises which give you a chance to practise Greek alphabetical order. Most words in Greek dictionaries are written in lower case letters, so there are many occasions when you will have to switch from capitals to lower case if you want to look them up. The words you find on road signs, in cartoons or newspaper headlines, for instance, are usually written in capitals. But first of all, here is the Greek alphabet again, on page 134, with the letter names written alongside. You don't have to learn the names in order to use a dictionary, but you may find that it helps you to remember the order when you are looking up a word, if you can mutter the letters as you go along. As you can see, there are a few letters where the handwritten forms tend to be slightly different from the printed version. Also, note that the Greek ι, unlike its English counterpart, is not dotted. If you write the English form, *i*, the dot could be mistaken for a stress mark.

THE GREEK ALPHABET			
PRONUNCIATION	CAPITALS	LOWER CASE	HANDWRITTEN FORM
Alpha	A	α	α
Vita	B	β	β
Ghama	Γ	γ	γ
Thelta	Δ	δ	δ
Epsilon	E	ε	ε
Zita	Z	ζ	ζ
Ita	H	η	η
Thita	Θ	θ	θ
Yota	I	ι	ι
Kapa	K	κ	κ
Lamda	Λ	λ	λ
Mi	M	μ	μ
Ni	N	ν	ν
Xi	Ξ	ξ	ξ
Omikron	O	ο	ο
Pi	Π	π	π
Rho	P	ρ	ρ
Sigma	Σ	σ, ς	ς
Taf	T	τ	τ
Ipsilon	Y	υ	υ
Fi	Φ	φ	φ
Hi	X	χ	χ
Psi	Ψ	ψ	ψ
Omega	Ω	ω	ω

Exercise 1

Fill in the missing letters of each sequence. If you need help, use the alphabet at the top of the page.

1   α – γ – ε – η – ι – λ – ν – ο – ρ – τ – φ – ψ –
2   – β – δ – ζ – θ – κ – μ – ξ – π – σ – υ – χ – ω

Now try to write out the Greek alphabet in lower case letters from α to θ. Check your answers using the alphabet at the top of the page. As soon as you can do that, try going a little further – maybe as far as π. Keep adding a few letters until you can make it all the way to ω. With that skill safely under your belt, repeat the process using capital letters.

Exercise 2

1   A – Γ – E – H – I – Λ – N – O – P – T – Φ – Ψ –
2   – B – Δ – Z – Θ – K – M – Ξ – Π – Σ – Y – X – Ω

Impress your friends!

If you have access to a computer, you can show off by signing your name in Greek characters every time you send an e-mail. The 'symbol' font in most computers changes the English letters on the keyboard to their Greek equivalents. Where there is no exact counterpart 'symbol' use spare English letters.

The English *Q* becomes the Greek θ, you press *H* for η, the English *y* is used for ψ, and your press *w* when you need ω.

Using a street map

A word that you will meet all the time is ΟΔΟΣ = STREET. In England you might find King Street, but in Greece, ΟΔΟΣ comes first, and it becomes Street of the King. Greek grammar changes the ending of king, but this shouldn't put you off striking out on your own to that little taverna that hardly anyone knows about, where they serve the most marvellous … but that would be telling! You'll just have to go and find out for yourself!

Using a dictionary

By now you have enough knowledge to be able to look up most of the words which you will meet on that idyllic trip to Greece, which we hope that you are planning. You may find, however, that, as in English, the word in the dictionary is not exactly the same as the one which you want. In English, for example, you won't find 'eaten' as a separate entry, although you will find 'eat'. This shouldn't be too much of a problem because it's usually the endings that may change for most of the words that you'll need to look up at this stage, so you'll probably be able to work out the meaning. We firmly believe that a dictionary is a journey rather than a destination. We hope you enjoy yours.

ΛΕΞΙΚΟ Dictionary

Α α

άγαλμα   statue

άγγελος   angel. It is also a Greek name, though less common now.

αγγίζω   I touch, I'm touching

Αγγλος   Englishman

αγορά   a market. Also 'a buy' as in 'I've made a buy' έκανα μία αγορά.

αγοράζω   I buy, I'm buying

αγορές   markets

αγγούρι   cucumber

άγουρο   unripe. Used for fruit and vegetables.

αεροπλάνο   aeroplane

Αθήνα   Athens

αίθριος   clement, usually referring to weather.

άκρη   edge

ακρόνυμο   acronym

Ακρόπολη   an influential Athenian daily paper. Also the 'edge' of a city; its highest part. Every ancient Greek city had an acropolis, though the one most famous now is the one in Athens.

αλάτι   salt, also seen as αλας on some packets of salt.

Αμερικάνικο   American (adjective)

Αμερική   America

αμόκ   amok

ανάγραμμο anagram
Απογευματηνή initially a daily newspaper appearing only in Athens
  (as most papers did at the time), it's now a national paper.
αρτοπωλείο bakery
άρτος bread. Old Greek.
ασπιρίνη aspirin. This is a compound word for white (άσπρη) and
  fiery (πυρίνη).
άστατος unsettled
ακατάστατος untidy
άτομο atom, individual
αυγά eggs
Αυστραλία Australia
αυτοκίνητο car

Β β

βάζο vase
βάζω I put, I'm putting
βανίλλια vanilla
Βέσπα small motorcycle or Vespa
βιβλίο (βιβλία) book(s)
βιβλιοπωλείο bookshop
βούτηρο butter
βροχή rain

Γ γ

γάλα milk
γαλακτοπωλείο shop selling only dairy produce such as eggs, milk
  and yoghurt.
γεμιστά stuffed tomatoes (usually)
για for, about
γιαούρτι yoghurt. Greek yoghurt is usually made from either sheep or
  goat milk.
γιατί why, because
γκρίζο grey
γλυκά sweets (plural)
γλυκό sweet
γράμμα letter, both a letter of the alphabet and a letter one can post.
γραμματόσημα stamps

Δ δ

δέκα ten

δεκαεννέα nineteen, pronounced as δεκαεννέα or δεκαεννιά.

δεκαέξι sixteen

δεκαεπτά seventeen. Again, this one may be pronounced as either δεκαεπτά or δεκαεφτά

δεκαοκτώ eighteen, pronounced either as δεκαοκτώ or δεκαοχτώ

Δελφοί Delphi, famous oracle of Apollo.

δέμα parcel, packet

δεν not

δεξιά right

Δευτέρα Monday. In Greek it literally means the second day of the week.

Δημοτικό a Greek dance. It means popular or of the people. There are several regional types of 'popular' dances which come from different parts of Greece.

διαμέρισμα flat, apartment

δολλάριο dollar

δραχμή the Greek currency

δρόμος road

δύο two

δώδεκα twelve

δωδεκάνησα Dodecanese

δωμάτιο room

Ε ε

εδώ here

εισητήρια tickets

είσοδος entrance

εκατό a hundred

έλεος mercy

Ελευθεροτυπία one more of the Athenian newspapers

έλικας rotor blades

ελικόπτερο helicopter

Ελλάδα Greece

Ελληνικός (Ελληνικη, Ελληνικο) Greek. It is also the name by which Greek coffee, a potent brew, is known.

ένα   one
εννέα   nine. Its alternative is εννιά.
έξι   six
έξω   out
επάνω   up (older form of πανω)
επίλογος   epilogue. The last word, or conclusion of a work or play.
επτά   seven, or, alternatively, εφτά.
εστιατόρειο   restaurant
ευγένεια   politeness, also, quite literally, nobility.
ευγενής   noble, polite
ευγενικός   polite
εύκολο   easy
ευρό   Euro
ευχαριστώ   thank you
εφημερίδα   newspaper

Z ζ

ζάχαρη   sugar
ζαχαροπλαστείο   patisserie
ζελατίνα   jelly
ζέστη   heat
ζεστός   hot

H η

ηλιοθεραπεία   sunbathing
ήλιος   the sun

Θ θ

θέλω   I want
θεού   God's
θερμό   a thermos flask
θερμός   warm
Θερμοκρασία   temperature
θερμόμετρο   thermometer

I ι

Ιανουαρίου   January's

Ιαπωνία   Japan
ιδέα   idea
Ισπανική Πετσετα   the Spanish Peseta
Ιταλία   Italy
Ιταλική Λίρα   Italian Lira
Ιησούς   Jesus
ιχθύς   fish

Κ κ

καδένα   neck or watch chain, usually made of gold.
καζάνι   cauldron
και   and
κακό   bad
Καλαματιανό   Greek dance from the area of Kalamata.
κάνω   I do, I make/I'm doing, I'm making
καράβι   ship
καρότο   carrot
καρπούζι   water melon
καρτ-ποστάλ   postcard
κασέτα   cassette
καταιγίδα   storm
κάτω   down
καφέ   coffee, brown
καφέδες   coffees
καφενείο   the more traditional type of coffee shop. A kafenio is a very
   old concept. It is a predominantly men-only environment, and each
   has its own catchment area, much as a local pub in England would. It
   is not unusual for Greek men to spend all day in a kafenio, drinking
   ouzo and playing backgammon.
καφετερία   a coffee shop
κετσάπ   ketchup
κεφτεδάκια   small meatballs
κεφτέδες   meatballs
κεφτές   meatball. Also used as a derogatory word, i.e. to say someone
   is a 'meatball' is the equivalent of a 'butter-fingers' or also a
   'mummy's boy'.
κινηματογράφος   cinema. Literally translated, it means, 'writing in
   motion'.

κίνηση movement, as in motion. Also used to describe road traffic.
κίνημα movement, as in political faction.
κινητό mobile. Particularly useful when combined with the word
  'phone'.
Κλέφτικο a Greek dance
κόμμα comma (the punctuation mark)
Κορέα Korea
κοτόπουλο chicken
κρασί wine
Κρήτη Crete
Κρητικός a Cretan dance
κρίνος lily
κρίνω I judge, I'm judging
κριτής judge, critic
Κυριακή Sunday. Literally translated, it means the Lord's day.

Λ λ

λάδι oil. The term is applied equally to olive oil, sun-tan oil and
  motor oil.
λαός people massed together, and race, as in race of people.
λεμονάδα lemonade
λεμόνια lemons
λεωφορείο bus
Λονδίνο London

Μ μ

μαγαζί shop. This is applied in a generic manner to any shop
  in Greece.
Μαδρίτη Madrid
μακαρονάδα cooked spaghetti
μάξι a long skirt. The opposite of a mini skirt.
μαρούλι lettuce
μαρτίνι martini
με with
μεγάλα plural, big, large
μεγάλος big, large, old
μεζές tit bit
μενού menu

Μεσημεριανή originally an Athenian paper, now national (lit. noon paper). Others like it are; Σημεριανή (Today's paper), Κύρηκας (translated as the perhaps slightly ambitious 'Gospel') and Εθνική (National).

Μεξικό the city of Mexico

μήλα apples

μηλόπιττα apple pie

μικρά small, little (plural)

μίνι literally, the British cult car, but also a short skirt.

μόνο alone, only

μοσχαρήσια beef

μουσείο museum

μουστάρδα mustard

μπάρ bar. This is another imported word.

μπέικον bacon

μπισκότα biscuits

μπλουζάκι t-shirt

μπουκάλι bottle

μπουκάλια bottles

μπριζόλα steak

μπύρα beer

μπυραρία where you would go to drink beer and have a meze.

N ν

νερό water. The plural is νερα!

νότα a musical note

ντεντέκτιβ detective

ντισκοτέκ disco

ντομάτες tomatoes

Ξ ξ

ξενοδοχείο hotel

ξένος foreigner, stranger

O o

οδός street

οικονομία economy

οκταπόδι octopus. It may also be spelled as οχταπόδι and sometimes it's pronounced in the contracted form of χταπόδι. On menus it may appear in its diminutive of χταποδάκια (small octopi)

οκτώ eight. This can be pronounced as either οκτώ or οχτώ.

όλα all, everything

ομελλέτα omelette

ομίχλη fog

όμοιο the same, identical

ομόφωνη homophone

όνομα name

οπωροπολείο a fruit shop

Ουάσινγκτον the city of Washington DC

ουζερί a specialist outlet, traditionally cheap, where sailors and villagers would congregate to drink ouzo and listen to live music played on a mandolin.

ούζο the clear-coloured, fiery Greek drink which goes milky when water is added to it.

ουίσκυ whisky

Π π

πάγος ice

παγωτό ice-cream

πακέτο packet, parcel

πάνω up

παρακαλώ please

Παρασκεύη Friday. The word means 'day of preparation'.

Παρίσι Paris

Παστίτσιο a pasta and mincemeat dish whose origins lie more in the East than Greece.

πατατάκια crisps

πατάτες potatoes, chips

πάω I go, I'm going

Πελοπόννησος a regional newspaper. As the name suggests it is limited to the Peloponnese area.

Πέμπτη Thursday. Fifth day of the week.

πίνω I drink, I'm drinking

πιπέρι pepper

πίτσα pizza

πιτσαρία   the place where you would expect to buy a pizza.

πόλη   town, city

ποδήλατο   bicycle

πολιτική   politics

πολύ   very, a lot

πορτοκαλάδα   orangeade

πορτοκάλι   orange

ποτό   drink

πούλμαν   coach

πουλόβερ   pullover, sweater

P ρ

ρεκόρ   record (in sport, for example, rather than music)

Ρεμπέτικο   a Greek dance. The favourite of those who suffer from a 'heavy heart', rebetika are usually songs about abandonment and unfulfilment, and are accompanied by the mournful sound of the mandolin.

ρετσίνα   the famous Greek wine, which takes its name from the resin now used to flavour it.

Ρώσικο Ρούβλι   the Russian Rouble

Σ σ

Σάββατο   Saturday

σαγανάκι   traditionally ouzeri food. It consists of fried hard cheese and fried squid or octopus served in a light vinaigrette dressing.

σαλάτα   salad

Σάμος   the island of Samos

σάντουιτς   sandwich. The concept of the sandwich is relatively new in Greek culture and still considered something of a novelty in certain remote parts.

σήμα   sign, badge, signal

σημαία   flag

σιδηρόδρομος   railway

σίδηρος   iron

σόκ   shock. This is an imported word into Greek.

σοκολάτα   chocolate

σουβενίρ   souvenir

σοφία   wisdom. The old Greek church (now a mosque) in Istanbul is called *Agia Sofia* (Holy Wisdom).

σπόρ   sport

στο   at, in, or on, depending on usage and context.

συμπεριφορά   behaviour

συννεφιά   heavy cloud

Συρτάκι   a modern Greek dance

σως   sauce. Usually refers to tomato sauce.

σωτήρας   saviour

Τ τ

ταβέρνα   a traditional Greek restaurant

ταξί   taxi

ταξιδάκια   small trips or excursions

τάνξ   tank

ταχυδρομείο   post office

τελεφερίκ   cable car

Τετάρτη   Wednesday. Fourth day of the week.

τζατζίκι   a Greek garlic and yoghurt dip.

τζίπ   jeep. The American make of car which took its name from the cartoon character. In Greek it refers generically to most four-wheel drive vehicles.

τηγανητές   fried (usually refers to chips).

τεκίλα   tequila

τομή   a cut, usually along a premarked line

τόξο   bow (as in 'bow and arrow')

τραίνο   train

τριμμενο   grated

Τρίτη   Tuesday. Third day of the week.

τρόποι   manners, method, way

τρόποι συμπεριφοράς   manners (literally, way of behaviour)

τρώμε   we eat, we are eating

τσάντα   handbag

τυρί   cheese

τυροπωλείο   a shop specialising in the sale of cheese

Υ υ

υιός   formal Greek for son

υποβρύχιο   submarine

Φ φ

φαγητό   food

φαρμακείο   pharmacy, chemist

φάστ φούντ   fast food

φεριμπότ   ferry (boat)

φέτα   a soft, white Greek cheese, made out of goat's milk, with a distinctive flavour and texture.

φίλη   a female friend

φίλμ   movie, film

φίλος   a masculine friend

φορτηγό   truck

φούρνου   oven baked. Quite a lot of food is cooked that way in Greece.

φρούτα   fruit

φρουτοπωλείο   a place where you would go to buy fresh fruit and vegetables.

φύλο   sex (M and F)

φωνή   voice

φωτογραφία   photograph

X χ

χάμπουρκερ   hamburger

χάρτης   map

χαρτί   paper

χείρα   hand (formal)

χήρα   widow

χίλια   a thousand

χιόνι   snow

χοίρα   sow, i.e. female pig

χοιρινή   pork

χορός   dance

χωριάτικη   usually known as Greek salad, though the more literal translation is 'village salad'.

Χριστός   Christ

χρυσός   gold

χρυσοχοείο   a jeweller's

χρυσόψαρο   goldfish
χρυσοθήρας   gold digger

Ψ ψ

ψάρι   fish
ψαροπωλείο   a fishmonger's
ψωμί   bread
ψώνια   the shopping
ψωνίζω   I buy, I am buying

Ω ω

ωμέγα   omega, the final letter of the Greek alphabet.
ώρα   time
ωραία   nice

ENGLISH–GREEK VOCABULARY

about για
acronym ακρόνυμο
acropolis Ακρόπολη
aeroplane αεροπλάνο
afternoon απόγευμα
alone μόνο
America Αμερική
American Αμερικάνικο (An
  American person is either
  Αμερικανός (m.) or
  Αμερικανίδα (f.))
amok αμόκ
anagram ανάγραμμο
and και
angel άγγελος
apple pie μηλόπιττα
apples μήλα
aspirin ασπιρίνη
at στο
Athens Αθήνα
atom άτομο
Australia Αυστραλία

bacon μπείκον
bad κακό
badge σήμα
baked φούρνου
bakery αρτοπωλείο
bar μπάρ
because γιατί
beef μοσχαρήσια
beer μπύρα

behaviour συμπεριφορά
bicycle ποδήλατο
big μεγάλος (s.) μεγάλα (pl.)
biscuits μπισκότα
book βιβλίο
bookshop βιβλιοπωλείο
bottle μπουκάλι
bottles μπουκάλια
bow (as in bow and arrow) τόξο
bread άρτος (old Greek), ψωμι
brown καφέ
bus λεωφορείο
butter βούτηρο
buy: I am buying = ψωνίξω,
  αγοραζω (Also 'a buy' as in
  'I've made a buy'. εκανα μια
  αγορά.)

cable car τελεφερίκ
car αυτοκίνητο
carrot καρότο
cassette κασέτα
cauldron καζάνι
cheese τυρί
chicken κοτόπουλο
chips πατάτες
chocolate σοκολάτα
Christ Χριστός
cinema κινηματογράφος
clement (weather) αίθριος
cloud συννεφιά
coach πούλμαν

coffee καφέ
coffee shop καφετερία (The more traditional type of coffee shop is a καφενείο)
coffees καφέδες
comma κόμμα
Crete Κρήτη
crisps πατατάκια
cucumber αγγούρι
cut (noun), usually along a pre-marked line τομή

dairy, i.e. a shop selling only dairy produce γαλακτοπωλείο
dance χορός
Delphi, famous oracle of Apollo Δελφοί
detective ντέντεκτιβ
disco ντισκοτέκ
do: I'm doing = κάνω
Dodecanese Δωδεκάνησα. Greek islands of the Aegean (literally, twelve islands, although only the major ones have a permanent population and some of the smaller ones are used only for fishing or keeping sheep on.)
dollar δολλάριο
down κάτω
drachma δραχμή
drink ποτό
    I'm drinking πίνω

easy εύκολο
eat: we are eating = τρώμε
economy οικονομία
edge άκρη
eggs αυγά
eight οκτώ, οχτώ
eighteen δεκαοκτώ, δεκαοχτώ
Englishman Αγγλος
entrance είσοδος

epilogue επίλογος
Euro ευρό
excursions ταξιδάκια
exit έξοδος

fast food φάστ φούντ
ferry boat φεριμπότ
fiery πύρινη
fish ιχθύς, ψάρι
fishmonger's ψαροπωλείο
flag σημαία
fog ομίχλη
food φαγητό
for για
foreigner ξένος
Friday Παρασκευή
fried (usually refers to chips) τηγανητές
friend φίλος (m.), φίλη (f.)
fruit φρούτα
fruit shop οπωροπολείο

God's θεού
go: I'm going = πάω
gold χρυσός
gold digger χρυσοθήρας
goldfish χρυσόψαρο
Greece Ελλάδα
Greek (adj.) Ελληνικός (A Greek person is Ελληνας (m.) or Ελληνίδα (f.))
grey γκρίζο

hamburger χάμπουρκερ
handbag τσάντα
heat ζέστη
helicopter ελικόπτερο
here εδώ
homophone ομόφωνη
hot ζεστό
hotel ξενοδοχείο
hundred εκατό

ice πάγος
ice cream παγωτό
idea ιδέα
identical όμοιο
important μεγάλος (s.), μεγάλα (pl.)
in στο
individual άτομο
iron σίδηρο
Italian Ιταλική
Italy Ιταλία

January's Ιανουαρίου
Japan Ιαπωνία
jeep τζίπ
jelly ζελατίνα
Jesus Ιησούς
jeweller's (shop) χρυσοχοείο
judge, critic κριτής
judge: I'm judging = κρίνω

ketchup κέτσαπ
Korea Κορέα

lemonade λεμονάδα
lemons λεμόνια
letter (both a letter of the alphabet and
    a letter one can post) γράμμα
lettuce μαρούλι
lily κρίνος
Lira Λίρα
London Λονδίνο
lot, many πολύ

Madrid Μαδρίτη
make: I'm making = κάνω
manners (literally, way of behaviour)
    τρόποι συμπεριφοράς
map χάρτης
market αγορά
markets αγορές
martini μαρτίνι
maxi μάξι
meatballs κεφτέδες (Small meatballs
    are κεφτεδάκια.)

menu μενού
mercy έλεος
method τρόποι
Mexico Μεξικό
milk γάλα
mini (the British cult car or a short
    skirt) μίνι
mobile κινητό (Particularly useful
    when combined with the word
    τηλέφωνο 'phone'.)
Monday Δευτέρα
movement (political faction) κινημα,
    (road traffic) κίνηση
movie, film φίλμ
museum μουσείο
mustard μουστάρδα

name όνομα
neck chain, usually made of gold
    καδένα
newspaper εφημερίδα
nine εννέα, εννιά
nineteen δεκαεννέα, δεκαεννιά
nobility ευγένεια
noble ευγενής
not δεν
note (musical) νότα

octopus οκταπόδι, οχταπόδι,
    χταποδάκια (small octopi)
oil λάδι
old μεγάλος
omega, the final letter of the Greek
    alphabet ωμεγα (Also used as a
    symbol for the last word in
    anything, for example, the Omega
    theory in cosmology about the end
    of time and omega particles in
    physics which are the final products
    of experiments in cyclotrons
    (particle accelerators).)
omelette ομελέτα
on στο

one ένα
only μόνο
orange πορτοκάλι
orangeade πορτοκαλάδα
out έξω
ouzo ούζο
oven φούρνος

packet πακέτο, δέμα
paper χαρτί
parcel πακέτο, δέμα
Paris Παρίσι
pâtisserie ζαχαροπλαστείο
people (race) λαός
pepper πιπέρι
Peseta πετσέτα
pharmacy, chemist φαρμακείο
photograph φωτογραφία
pizza πίτσα
please παρακαλώ
polite ευγενικός, ευγενής
politeness ευγένεια
  (literally, nobility)
politics πολιτική
pork χοιρινή
postcard καρτ-ποστάλ
post office ταχυδρομείο
potatoes πατάτες
pullover πουλόβερ
put: I'm putting = βάζω

race (of people) λαός
railway σιδηρόδρομος
record (for example, in sport) ρεκόρ
restaurant εστιατόρειο
retsina ρετσίνα
right δεξιά
road δρόμος
room δωμάτιο
rotor blades έλικας
Rouble Ρούβλι

salad σαλάτα

salt αλάτι, άλας
same όμοιο
Samos Σάμος
sandwich σάντουιτς
Saturday Σάββατο
sauce (usually refers to tomato sauce)
  σως
saviour σωτήρας
seven εφτά, επτά
seventeen δεκαεπτά, δεκαεφτά
sex φύλο
ship καράβι
shock σόκ
shop μαγαζί
shopping ψώνια
sign, signal σήμα
six έξι
sixteen δεκαέξι
small, little μικρός (s.), μικρά (pl.)
snow χιόνι
son γιος, υιος (formal Greek)
souvenir σουβενίρ
sow, i.e. female pig χοίρα
spaghetti (cooked) μακαρονάδα
Spanish Ισπανική
sport σπορ
stamps γραμματόσημα
statue άγαλμα
steak μπριζόλα
storm καταιγίδα
stranger ξένος
street οδός
stuffed (usually stuffed tomatoes)
  γεμιστά
submarine υποβρύχιο (In Greece it
  is also used to refer to oblong pizzas
  intended only for one. They're
  called pizza subs!)
sugar ζάχαρη
sun ήλιος
sunbathing ηλιοθεραπεία

Sunday Κυριακή (literally, the
  Lord's day)
sweater πουλόβερ
sweet γλυκό
sweets γλυκά
tank τάνξ
taxi ταξί
temperature θερμοκρασία
ten δέκα
tequila τεκίλα
thank you ευχαριστώ
thermometer θερμόμετρο
thermos flask θερμό
thousand χίλια
thousands χιλιάδες
tickets εισητήρια
time ώρα
tit bit μεζές
tomatoes ντομάτες
touch: I'm touching = αγγίζω
town, city πόλη
train τραίνο
truck φορτηγό
t-shirt μπλουζάκι
Tuesday Τρίτη
twelve δώδεκα
two δύο

unripe άγουρο

unsettled άστατος
untidy ακατάστατος
up πάνω, επάνω

vanilla βανίλλια
vase βάζο
very πολύ
Vespa (small motorcycle) Βέσπα
voice φωνή

want, I θέλω
warm θερμός
Washington DC Ουάσινγκτον
watch chain καδένα
water νερό, νερά (pl.)
water-melon καρπούζι
way τρόποι
Wednesday Τετάρτη
whisky ουίσκυ
white άσπρο
why γιατί
widow χήρα
wine κρασί
wisdom σοφία
with με

xylophone ξυλόφωνο (literally,
  'voice of wood')

yoghurt γιαούρτι